The Christian
DIFFERENCE

should be visible in all we do. Hugh Silvester, rector of Holy Trinity, Platt's Lane, Manchester, shows how the Christian life can be lived at the personal, church and world levels

HUGH SILVESTER

The Christian DIFFERENCE

Foreword by The Bishop of Rochester

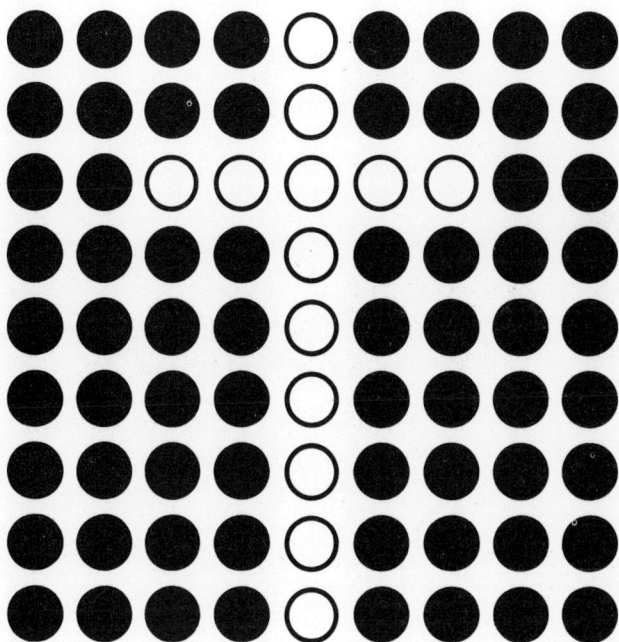

FALCON

London

FALCON

A FALCON BOOK

published by
Church Pastoral Aid Society
Falcon Court, 32 Fleet Street, London, EC4Y 1DB

distributed overseas by
Australia: EMU Book Agencies Ltd, 63 Berry Street, Granville, 2142, NSW
New Zealand: Scripture Union Bookshop, PO Box 760, Wellington

The Christian
DIFFERENCE

ISBN 0 85491 535 4
First published 1977
Text © Hugh Silvester

DESIGNED AND PRODUCED IN THE UNITED KINGDOM
Photoset in Baskerville type and bound by
Richard Clay (The Chaucer Press) Ltd, Bungay, Suffolk
Printed offset litho by
Fletcher & Son Ltd, Norwich, Norfolk

contents

Foreword *The Bishop of Rochester* *page*

To the reader 9

1 **A personal commitment** 11

2 **A group commitment** 22

3 **A world commitment** 34

4 **Law and grace** 43

5 **Expecting nothing in return** 57

6 **The world's squeeze** 68

7 **Led by the Spirit** 79

8 **His Spirit is with us** 90

9 **Filled with the Spirit** 101

Foreword

Today, we are continually being told that the Church is faced not with a crisis of cash but with a crisis of commitment. The knocking away, one by one, of the props which hitherto supported conventional church life has not only revealed the minority status of Christians in society, but it has also sharpened the difference between Christians and their neighbours. For many, especially those setting out on the Christian pilgrimage, this raises questions concerned with the faith and the life of the follower of Christ.

Hugh Silvester, whom I had the pleasure of ordaining at my first ordination in 1961, sets out in this book to help his readers discover the true nature of commitment to Christ and to membership of his world-wide Church. He draws on his experience of working with young people in a Kent parish and in colleges in Uganda and North London. His approach is essentially biblical and sacramental and he is careful to make explicit the background of scripture against which he writes from his own convinced standpoint.

I am sure that many young people, as well as some not so young, will be helped by this book to deepen their Christian discipleship. I hope they may also be prompted to take more seriously the world of men and nations in which Christians are called to live and to serve, as well as to seek to understand patiently and lovingly the needs and aspirations of those from whom they know themselves to be different.

Rochester

Bishop of Rochester (Dr David Say)

To the reader

It was late one night in one of the exhibition halls in Brussels. I had been having a discussion with a group of young Swedish Christians when one of the girls suddenly said, 'What I have learnt at EURO-FEST is that you cannot separate love and truth.'

That's it: that's the big one. Love and truth go together for both of them come from God. People try to separate them with disastrous results. Until about twenty years ago there were large numbers of Christians in the West who were very good at truth but not very good at love. The result was a dry, 'we know all about it,' joyless religion. All very correct but cold as the grave.

Then there was a reaction, mostly among young people but not restricted to them. They rediscovered the promises about a joyful, daily experience with God. I say 'rediscovered' because it would be absurd to suggest that they invented it. But strangely this great emphasis on loving experience with Jesus and his Church has led to a neglect of truth. This book is mainly about the unchanging truth of Christianity. This does not mean it has nothing to do with everyday life: God's truth is something to be *lived*.

Every new Christian needs the truth. First, it will help you to understand your experience of Jesus and not to misapply it to others. Secondly, it will open up to you new experiences in learning from others. It is obvious that we are all different sorts of people and yet we must agree if we are to be one in Christ. And what we agree in is the truth. If love is based merely on trying to be nice to one another then sooner or later it will become superficial and shortlived.

There are several ways in which you can use this book:

● Read it straight through and see how believing the truth of God will give you a different life-style of love.

● Work through it again with your Bible, using the verses written out at the end of each chapter and mark the verses in your Bible.

● Get three or four friends to read it at the same time and take it a chapter a time. Meet for an evening, say every week, discussing the questions at the end of the chapter and bringing out further truths on your own.

NOTE TO THOSE UNUSED TO LOOKING UP VERSES IN THE BIBLE

Each reference is made up of book, chapter and verse. So, 'Acts 1:8' means:

> The book of Acts
> Chapter 1
> Verse 8

If you do not have a Bible of your own I suggest in the first place that you get *Good News for Modern Man*. Most of the quotations in this book are taken from this translation which is known as Today's English Version (TEV). Any other versions used are shown in the following way:

RSV   Revised Standard Version of the Bible
      (in some editions called *The Common Bible*)
NEB   New English Bible
JBP   J. B. Phillips's translation of the New Testament

You should have a whole Bible as soon as possible and I suggest you get the RSV for serious study as it keeps close to the original languages in which the Scriptures were written.

Manchester   **Hugh Silvester**

I

A personal commitment

ONLY ONE TRUTH

There are many ways into the Christian faith but there is only one faith when you get there. Some people come to Christ out of a great sense of need, a 'spiritual' need like that of forgiveness or a 'physical' need like desperately needing somewhere to live. Others grow into faith, you might almost say drift into faith, as they accept the standards and the way of life of Christian parents or youth leaders. And yet others argue their way into faith as they try and answer questions that have been troubling them for years like 'What am I here for?'

But there is only one faith. And this is because there is only one God who is the Father of our Lord Jesus Christ. It is important to be clear about this. It is obvious to say that each person is unique and we are right to reject firmly the idea that all Christians should be carbon copies of each other. Straight-jacketing of characters is to violate both God's work of creation (no one else has *your* chromosomes) and God's work of redemption (described by Peter as 'many-coloured grace'). But we should not be misled into thinking that because we are all unique that God is different for each person. He is not variable and although the *form* of our experience of God will differ vastly from one another, the *content* of our experience will be the same.

Let me illustrate what I mean by this contrast between *form* and *content*. Let us take the Christian virtue of patience. One Christian may be, say, a schoolgirl whose form mistress is particularly malicious towards her. Another may be a middle-aged man who is hen-pecked at home. The make-up of these two Christians and their experience of God are, in *form*, totally different and yet the *content* of the Christian life in these two very different people is the same. They must both learn to suffer patiently under unjust treatment. And the reason why the content is the same is because they both owe a personal allegiance to the same Christ. And it is because of what Christ did ('Think of what he went through, how he put up with so much hatred from sinful men!') that the demand made by God on these two Christians is the same.

In this book I shall try to outline what it is that all Christians have in common. Of course, most of the real life illustrations will be drawn from my own western culture and if I succeed at all, it will mostly be with those who share that culture. But this 'sameness' of the Christian life is something which has not changed through two thousand years of Christian experience in many different cultures. Another more traditional name for this 'sameness' is 'doctrine' or 'teaching.' Not some kind of theoretical information but health-giving teaching which will make the Christian sound in wind and mind. So we must study the *truth* of the Christian life if we are to be truly Christian. Jesus was always driving this point home with his favourite 'Truly, truly I say to you . . .' a formula recorded twenty-five times in John's gospel alone.

And most of this truth is about God. Of course the Bible does have something to say about man but this is not the heart of the matter. It is the nature of God – his actions, his purposes and his intentions for us – which is of absorbing importance. Without that knowledge there is nothing 'different' about the Christian. No doubt Jesus has a number of valuable insights about man's life and attitudes but if he is not telling us truth about God then where shall we find a real basis for life? This is the supernaturalism of Jesus that he can bring people into real contact with God. If he cannot do that, then he is merely another peddler of proverbs.

THE TRUTH MAKES A DIFFERENCE

Becoming a Christian makes a difference. It makes a man different from what he was: and it makes him different from those around him. But where does the difference lie? Is it possible to describe it? It is tempting to say that it lies in a changed style of living but while this should undoubtedly be true it is not the starting-point. Becoming a different sort of person is an integral part of the 'difference' but it is not the mainspring of the Christian's understanding:

that would be far too man-centred. The driving force of the Christian's approach to life is the *fact* that he has a real relationship to God, a genuine link with the *greatest person that there is*. And it is this fact which makes a difference in the Christian's life-style. This link is forged by God himself and it is founded on a mutual commitment. God has committed himself to me and I have committed myself to God.

GOD IS COMMITTED TO ME

Let us first see what it means to say that 'God has committed himself to me.' God's nature is love. So Jesus taught and so we believe. And yet no one has seen God, so how can we possibly know what he is like? This is a real difficulty and one that we should face squarely. How is it possible to say that God is such and such when his being is quite unlike any other kind of being? Our very language which is fashioned from human conversation seems quite inadequate even to talk about him without making him a kind of human person. Jesus's answer to the problem is startlingly simple, 'God is my Father,' he said. 'Before the world was, I shared his glory, so if you have seen me you have seen him.' It is possible for us to know God because he has committed himself to us in the person of Jesus Christ. Now if this is true it is easy to see why Christians refuse to regard Christianity as merely 'one of the great world religions.' If Jesus's claim is correct then Christianity is not just one way of looking at God, it is the real thing. For some, this claim is a real offence as it is thought to make God partial, favouring one section of the race only. But the point to seize hold of is that unless the Incarnation (God becoming man) did happen, we can know nothing about the inner nature of God. So we might say God committed himself to me at Christmas, so that I could see him and know him.

But then God committed himself to me also on Good Friday. The cross of Jesus is the next evidence of his commitment. Jesus did not come to the earth to be a spectator giving good advice from the sidelines. He identified himself completely with those who needed him most. We have in the gospels a delightful portrait of a good man freely and unpatronisingly spending time with bad men and women. He was called 'friend of sinners' and it was meant to be an insult. Instead he transformed that nickname into a name of great purpose and compassion and it is a title that has wide implications for us now. For it is on the cross that we see Jesus taking his nickname to its full, logical conclusion. We see him grappling bare-handed with all the horror of human sin and betrayal and it killed him. And the Scriptures and the creeds say that he did it 'for me.' Two small words, which speak of the depths of God's commitment to us. He is so concerned, so involved that he will hold nothing back which would be for our benefit.

But we still have not reached the end of God's commitment to us. For having done all that was necessary to put the wrong right, he then completed his work with the offer of his Holy Spirit through the promise of the risen Jesus. It is impossible to exaggerate the immensity of this promise, because the Holy Spirit is God himself! I can only guess at what it must cost the *Holy* Spirit to live intimately in the life of a *sinful*, unclean and rebellious man. But it is a cost which God daily and gladly pays. Small wonder that Paul warns us not to grieve God's Holy Spirit for it must be easier for selfish men to grieve him rather than please him. And yet Jesus says, 'How much more, then, the Father in heaven will give the Holy Spirit to those who ask him.' The Old Testament is full of promises like 'I will never leave you nor forsake you' and these are repeated in the New Testament. Whatever we do, God will not be driven away! He is the relentless lover, willing to pay any price to fulfil his commitment.

Now if we ask the question, 'Why should God bother about me? Why should God be committed to me?', we can see that the direction of the answer will lie in the very *constitution* of God. It is not that he chooses to reveal himself as Father, Son and Holy Spirit; it is that he *is* Father, Son and Holy Spirit. This is the name of God for that is what he is, the God of commitment. To use the Bible word, he is the God of the 'Covenant.' He has bound himself, pledged himself to us and he will not go back on his promise. Here, then, is the beginning of Christian truth: it is the revelation of what God is, outgoing and committed to me. And each 'person' of the Trinity has his special part in assuring me that God is, really and truly, reaching out to me in love. Once you believe that, you are beginning to be different.

MY COMMITMENT TO GOD
We now come to what many mistakenly put first, 'my personal commitment' to God. Far too many young Christians try to build a

whole lifetime on what I like to call 'decision theology.' This is the kind of thinking where 'my decision' comes first and is made the basis of all that follows. Very often what happens is that after a few months the new convert finds that he is as big a sinner as he was before (if not worse!) and draws the quite incorrect conclusion that his commitment wasn't sincere enough and that what he now needs is 'deeper dedication' or 'total surrender.' 'Oh yes,' I hear people say, 'I gave my life to Christ but I didn't really understand it and two years later I gave my *whole* life to Christ.' No, of course he didn't understand it, nor does he understand now! What he needs to get hold of is that the important thing about his commitment is the nature of the God to whom he is committed not the nature or depth of his own response. Of course hypocrisy is not a real response. But our response will always be weak compared to the enormous offers God makes to us daily.

But now I have said that and got the priorities straight then, of course, if we are to enjoy God's offers, we must be prepared to enter into a deep commitment to him. And this commitment must be a 'whole-life' commitment. Look at these words of Jesus:

If anyone wants to come with me, he must forget himself, take up his cross every day, and follow me. For whoever wants to save his own life will lose it; but whoever loses his life for my sake will save it.   *Luke 9:23, 24*

Notice the uncompromising demand. For Jesus is in effect saying this, 'My commitment to you is total. I am prepared to lay down everything for your sake. I will even go to the cross to rescue you. Would you do the same for me? I promise you, you won't regret it if you do, but it will be exceedingly costly.' What Jesus is asking for is a re-centring of our lives. Our whole earthy, 'normal' nature is self-centred and he is asking us to 'forget it' or as the New English Bible puts it 'You must leave self behind.' It is as though you had all your wealth in a bank account and God asked you to sign a book of blank cheques in his favour. Now, in principle, God could within twenty-four hours fill in one of the cheques for the whole amount. That very evening you could be called on to die as a martyr. In practice, God presents his cheques little by little, laying his finger on first this decision ('Give me time by praying daily') and then on that friendship ('You are far too easily persuaded by him') and so on until we begin to understand that we really did offer him the whole of our lives to be a 'living sacrifice.' But very few of us see the end from the beginning. How could we? And if we could see, how many of us would have the courage to decide to put God first? My experience is that God *does* make demands but patiently and graciously so that we are ready when the moment comes.

I spoke recently to a vicar who described how he and his wife were once driving through a most unattractive town. They said to each other, 'We could never come here; it would be ghastly.' Then some years later God *did* call them to that very place. They found to their surprise they could not only take the decision to move but really enjoyed it when they got there.

A WHOLE-LIFE COMMITMENT

Let us look at this phrase 'whole-life' from another angle. Man is not just a simple being and that's that. He has many strands to his being. One way of dividing up or classifying man's diverse activity is to talk of feeling, intellect and will. Each of these aspects of man's life must be included in any 'whole-life' commitment.

First then, *feelings*. In general people think a lot of their bodies and the demands they make. It is possible to get so much pleasure from the body that it is not surprising that the pursuit of pleasure becomes the main concern in life. Then a person becomes a Christian. He discovers there is more to life than food and drink and sport. He discovers the 'dimension' of the spiritual and he is thrilled. But then he sometimes makes a mistake: he imagines that God is not concerned with the body which is considered to be 'only physical' and thinks that as a Christian all he has to do is to give God his due in the things of the spirit. Paul corrects this mistake. 'Use your bodies for God's glory,' he says. All feelings must be committed to God.

There are the very basic feelings of the body like appetite, heat, cold, physical fear. All these need to be submitted to the discipline of Christ. Most people in the West eat too much: are you willing to submit your appetite to Christ? Do you complain of the cold? Do you stop working in hot weather? For many years I had a poor head for heights and when a friend invited me to climb a mountain with him in Kenya I was afraid. But I wanted to go and I decided to trust Christ to see me through. I submitted my fears to him. In the course of my daily Bible reading I came across a promise in Romans 8 that neither height nor depth could separate me from his love. It was God's word to me at that moment. So I went on the expedition and he set me free. Trivial? Selfish? No, I don't think so; he is interested in my whole life.

But then there are the more complex, hard-to-reach feelings like anxiety and guilt and longing for sexual experience. Can these be committed to God? Look at the story of the Lost Son in Luke 15 and see how the father understood the young boy's longing to do his own thing and show everybody. And how those feelings of remorse and repentance were so perfectly dealt with as soon as they were committed by a faith expecting the father's relentless love! Or take the story in Luke 7 of the woman who lived a sinful life. She poured out her feelings on Jesus with tears and kisses expressing her repentance in an unashamed way. How warmly Jesus commends her! He speaks the word of forgiveness and praises her for her faith. She is assured by his acceptance, made to feel valuable.

One of our strongest feelings is the need for security. It is not so obvious as our hunger for food nor is it a bodily feeling like our desire for sex. It is a feeling that we are not complete in ourselves and that we need something more permanent and stronger than ourselves to lean upon. We do all kinds of things to cover up our lack of security like building large bank balances. For many people, getting married helps to provide them with a sense of security. But in spite of all these compensations we still feel insecure and this is because we are created beings. We can only find a permanent security by turning to God and putting our whole trust in him. This 'feeling' like the others must be committed to God.

Secondly, the *intellect*. It is a continual source of distress to Christian teachers that so many young Christians seem to lock their intellect up into a 'work' compartment and try to survive in the 'Christian bit' of their lives by devotional reading, fervent language and one or two dramatic (and sometimes imagined) answers to prayer. Intellect, of course, covers far more than sheer academic activity. When a man becomes a Christian he starts to 'read' life differently, he has different priorities, different values. He starts to see life as God sees it and so begins to acquire that rare and valuable commodity, 'wisdom.' But this does not happen all of a sudden by a miracle. Intellectual activity has its painstaking side: learning, memorising, summarising, articulating, arguing, thinking. All these should be committed to God.

Some new Christians object to the intellectual side of the

Christian life. They say 'Surely the Christian life is all above love. We don't want to start making it boring and something you do out of books. It is meant to be warm and real.' Like all objections this attitude has sense in it: if we do not become loving then our Christianity is worth nothing. But what is the basis of Christian love? It is Christian truth. *It is true* that Christ 'died for our sins' and understanding the scope of that will show us how much he loves us. *It is true* that Christians are all members of the one body and so should love each other. *It is true* that men without Christ are missing the best so it is the loving thing to go and speak to them of Christ's offer. So love is based on truth and truth is grasped by study: intellectual study, however simple in the first place.

As a basic start the Christian should be doing regular, thoughtful Bible study, recording his results in a note-book, sharing his discoveries with friends. But there are other books and magazines to be read; there are arguments to be contested; there are films to be criticised and political policies to be assessed. All this and much more will take place as you seriously commit your intellect to God.

If you leave out the intellectual component of the Christian life then sooner or later you will suffer for it. In the first place you will be unable to answer the objections of worldly friends and although you may cling to your experience ('I know it's true because I feel better') the doubts they sow in your mind will inevitably grow over the years. But the real threat is when life itself hits you; when the pressure is on; when illness comes or bereavement weakens you; when you lose your job; when your best friend betrays you. It is then that you need a secure faith. It will probably not help you then to rely on feelings of peace or forgiveness or guidance, for you feel dreadful. No, it is then that you must be able to say to yourself 'I know it is true and I shall continue to believe it.'

And then, thirdly, and perhaps most obviously, the *will*. Again and again there come times when the feelings are weak or antagonistic, when the arguments seem superficial or lack conviction. And then God appeals directly to our will and says 'Will you do what I say, simply because I say it?' And we must answer 'yes' if it is a whole-life commitment. It is not easy to do this. Nothing makes us rebel quicker than being treated like children and yet relative to God we *are* children. *We* cannot know what is best for us. But God knows and we should do what he says. Obedience to God and his revealed will in the Bible is an essential part of your commitment.

It is not that you hope to earn merit by doing what he says (and we will discuss this further in Chapter 4); it is simply that obedience is the logical conclusion of repentance and faith.

Take repentance. To a child who has offended, we say 'Are you sorry? Then don't do it again.' If he does do it again we say, 'There, you were not really sorry.' Or take faith. To a boy using a chisel for the first time, we say 'Keep both hands behind the cutting edge.' Ten minutes and two Elastoplasts later we conclude he does not believe us that the maxim is a sound one. 'Oh, but I *do* believe you,' says the boy. 'Then do what I say' is the logical rejoinder. Obedience is not an extra to repentance and faith but the practical expression of repentance and faith.

Paul points out in his letter to the Ephesian church that becoming a Christian is a bit like getting married. The heart of the marriage ceremony is the challenge to the *will*. The clergyman in church does not say to the bride, 'Do you feel that this man is a nice chap?' Nor does he say, 'Write an essay on the value of marriage.' The question is, '*Will* you take this man to be your wedded husband?' This act of will then has to be sustained right through life in all kinds of changing circumstances. So with the Christian. God often gives us wonderful feelings and he shows his truth to us. But in the end he says, '*Will* you?', and if you say, 'Yes,' then the promise is a whole-life commitment, that is for all time.

A PERSONAL COMMITMENT

The Christian neglects or overlooks any portion of his life in relation to God at his peril. We are *whole* men and God is God of the body, the spirit, the soul and all is to be committed to him, the whole human life that is you. The grounds for God's appeal is that he is already committed to you totally and has offered to bind up his whole life with yours. So the Christian difference is a personal commitment. It is not an arid, abstract philosophy; it is to do with warm living people. It is personal because you must do it yourself and another cannot do it for you. It is personal because it involves a whole man and 'you' are in every part.

Bible quotations for Chapter 1

ONLY ONE TRUTH

There is one Lord, one faith, one baptism; there is one God and Father of all men, who is Lord of all. *Ephesians 4:5, 6*

Let us give thanks to the God and Father of our Lord Jesus Christ, the merciful Father, the God from whom all help comes! *II Corinthians 1:3*

. . . faithful dispensers of the magnificently varied grace of God.

I Peter 4:10 (JBP)

Think of what he went through, how he put up with so much hatred from sinful men! So do not let yourselves become discouraged and give up. *Hebrews 12:3*

Jesus Christ is the same yesterday, today, and forever. *Hebrews 13:8*

THE TRUTH MAKES A DIFFERENCE

Hold to the true words that I taught you, as the example for you to follow and stay in the faith and love that are ours in union with Christ Jesus. *II Timothy 1:13*

GOD IS COMMITTED TO ME

No one has ever seen God. The only One, who is the same as God and is at the Father's side, he has made him known. *John 1:18*

But I am still full of confidence, for I know whom I have trusted, and I am sure that he is able to keep safe until that Day what he has entrusted to me.

II Timothy 1:12

Father; give me glory in your presence now, the same glory I had with you before the world was made. *John 17:5*

Whoever has seen me has seen the Father. Why, then, do you say 'Show us the Father'? *John 14:9*

CHRISTMAS

The Word was the source of life, and this life brought light to men. *John 1:4*

. . . you say 'Look at him! a glutton and a drinker, a friend of tax-gatherers and sinners!' *Luke 7:34 (NEB)*

GOOD FRIDAY

But God has shown us how much he loves us: it was while we were still sinners that Christ died for us. *Romans 5:8*

He did not even keep back his own Son, but offered him for us all! He gave us his Son – will he not also freely give us all things? *Romans 8:32*

PENTECOST

I dwell in the high and holy place and also with him who is of a contrite and humble spirit.   *Isaiah 57:15 (RSV)*

And do not grieve the Holy Spirit of God, for that Spirit is the seal with which you were marked.   *Ephesians 4:30 (NEB)*

I will not fail you or forsake you.   *Joshua 1:5 (RSV)*

I will never leave you; I will never abandon you.   *Hebrews 13:5*

If we are not faithful, he remains faithful, for he cannot be false to himself.
II Timothy 2:13

MY COMMITMENT TO GOD

I have been put to death with Christ on his cross, so that it is no longer I who live, but it is Christ who lives in me.   *Galatians 2.19, 20*

Offer yourselves as a living sacrifice to God, dedicated to his service and pleasing to him.   *Romans 12:1*

A WHOLE-LIFE COMMITMENT

May the God who gives us peace make you holy in every way, and keep your whole being, spirit, soul and body, free from all fault, at the coming of our Lord Jesus Christ.   *I Thessalonians 5:23*

(Saul) also talked and disputed with the Greek-speaking Jews, but they tried to kill him.   *Acts 9:29*

(Jesus said,) 'The right time has come and the Kingdom of God is near.'
Mark 1:15

Come near to God, and he will draw near to you.   *James 4:8*

Questions for discussion

1 Christmas – Good Friday – Pentecost. How far do these great festivals say all that needs to be said about the Christian faith?
2 How far is it good to follow your feelings?
3 'The reason you are not a Hindu is because you weren't born in India!' How would you meet this if challenged by a friend?

2

A group commitment

AN UNLIKELY CONVERSATION
I meet a violinist.

'Who do you play for?'

'I play at home.'

'But don't you admire the work of Sir Henry Beech?'

'Indeed I do. I have many of his records.'

'Then why don't you try and play in his orchestra?'

'Well, I did once but there was a man sitting next to me who used to clean his nails during the cadenzas.'

'But surely, that wouldn't affect the music!'

'You don't understand. I am a very sensitive person and I just love music. But I can't stand those people.'

'But don't you feel you're missing out by not making music with others?'

'Oh no. You see I have it all in my head and it's very beautiful. Besides all aesthetic experiences are truly subjective.'

'But you are a gifted person. Has it not crossed your mind that you are robbing the others by not joining an orchestra? After all there wouldn't be any records if there were no orchestras.'

'I don't think that matters. You see what I really enjoy is playing on my own.'

An absurd dialogue. No one, you say, would talk such nonsense. No, of course not – and that is because it is generally understood that making music is a corporate affair. It is something you do with other people. Yet it is not generally understood, even by Christians, that Christianity is a 'corporate affair.' There is, in all of us, a tendency to think of religion as something exclusively between me and God, whereas something which involves me with other people is 'social' life. This is the 'telephone box' view of the Church. I go to church in order to get through to God so that I may speak to him and hear him clearly speaking to me. All the other people, the clergy, the choir and the rest of the congregation are there to assist this dialogue between me and God. Often they distract me and when they do, the best thing is to clap my hands over my ears and concentrate on my devotions. After all there's only meant to be room for one in a telephone box.

Recently, there has been an interesting illustration of this point of view. With the arrival of the new services, some vicars have been encouraging the members of the congregation to turn and greet one another and shake hands and smile *during the service*. And some church members have been outraged. It is 'not reverent,' 'unsuitable,' 'distracting,' *etc.*, *etc.* This reaction is rooted in the notion that 'religious exercises' are between the individual and God and we must not interrupt them. You tend to find the same point of view held by those who come to 8 a.m. Holy Communion and nothing else. For at that service they will not be disturbed by singing or by a sermon and no one is very talkative at that time in the morning. So it is thought to be an ideal setting in which to get through to God.

A GROUP COMMITMENT

I am sure that a close study of the New Testament will show that such a view of the Church is distorted and will in turn distort those Christians who hold it. But before criticising the view let us notice that it contains a valuable truth. The Church is not merely a human institution or social club. It is a supernatural affair, rooted in God. And if a man 'comes to church' merely to have social contact, he will miss the main point which is to understand that the Church's business is with God. It is important that each worshipper should be concentrating on having communion with God but this should not blind him to the truth that God has called us into a group. Jesus himself used a number of metaphors to emphasise the corporate character of Christian experience. In John 10 he speaks of himself as the Good Shepherd caring for the sheep. Each sheep is known by name and follows him: that is the personal commitment. But then he goes on, 'There are other sheep that belong to me . . . I must bring them, too; they will listen to my voice and they will become one flock with one shepherd.' In the orchestra, each player has a vital link with the conductor and so becomes closely related to his fellow players. In a similar way each sheep with his dependence on the shepherd finds himself in a flock. His experience of the shepherd is found to be corporate.

Another metaphor Jesus uses is the vine and the branches. Each Christian is joined to Christ and draws his support from him. But he is therefore connected vitally to the other branches as the same life lives in each.

The teaching is even clearer in Paul's writing. Typical is the following passage:

> . . . you are now fellow-citizens with God's people and members of the family of God. You, too, are built upon the foundation laid by the apostles and prophets, the cornerstone being Christ Jesus himself. He is the one who holds the building together and makes it grow . . .
> *Ephesians 2:19–22*

Paul piles one picture on top of another: the city, the people, the family, the building and finally the body. The Church is the *body of Christ* – many members but one body. We are thus not only committed to Christ, but we are committed to one another in Christ. We learn from Christ indeed, but most of his teaching will come through other Christians. We serve Christ, certainly, but most of our service will be towards others. We love God, yes, but this love will be expressed in concern for our brother.

After all, think for a moment. How did you become a Christian? Was it not through Christians, members of the Church? Somebody spoke to you; somebody 'witnessed' to you; somebody preached to you. Who paid the preacher? Who trained him and taught him? Perhaps you became a Christian by reading the Bible. But who encouraged you? Who caused it to be printed? Who wrote it but fellow-Christians of long ago. Or perhaps you are that very rare bird, someone who was converted like Paul through a sudden direct disclosure from God. But who told you it was God-in-Christ revealing himself to you? And who instructed you further and baptised you by the command of Jesus? The answer to all these questions is 'the Church,' the body of Christ on earth directed by the Head who is in heaven. Imperfect though the Church is, it is nevertheless the focus of God's articulate work in the world. When you become a Christian then you become a 'sharer' in a group which is already committed to God.

FELLOWSHIP

One of Paul's favourite words is *koinonia* which literally means 'sharing.' In his letter to the Philippians the word comes three times. He speaks in 1:5 of Christians sharing in *the gospel*. The main thrust of this passage is that Paul is emphasising how the work he has done in preaching and evangelising is the work in which they have shared. But this sharing could not take place if Paul and his converts were not already sharers together of the benefits of the gospel. If you have recently become a Christian then your memory will still be vivid enough for you to delight in your new-found freedom. You still receive the word with joy. Well, then, you are not alone. You are not the only one to have tasted the gospel and found it to be good. You have begun a feast and you are not the only guest. Why not make friends with the others?

And then in Philippians 3:10 Paul speaks of 'sharing in *the suffer-ings* of Christ.' This is a most disturbing idea for we all shrink from suffering. The logic is straightforward enough, however. Christ has identified himself with us in suffering so that we might be free from sin. So if Jesus and I are committed each to the other, then I shall share *his* sufferings. I shall be involved in a love of a similar sort to his, a sacrificial love, a long-suffering love, an endless love. But this experience is something that I share with fellow-Christians. As Paul writes:

> For you have been given the privilege of serving Christ, not only by believing in him, but also by suffering for him. Now you can take part with me in the fight.
>
> *Philippians 1:29, 30*

And it is this 'fellowship of suffering' that strengthens me to bear what comes. Suffering for Christ, like believing the gospel, is a corporate affair and what strength lies here!

The third use talks of a sharing in *the* Holy Spirit:

> If then our common life in Christ yields anything to stir the heart, any loving consolation, any sharing of the Spirit, any warmth of affection or compassion, fill up my cup of happiness by thinking and feeling alike, with the same love for one another, the same turn of mind, and a common care for unity.
>
> *Philippians 2:1, 2 (NEB)*

Here is *the* reason why you cannot be a Christian on your own and why I reject the 'telephone box' view of the Church. It is because a Christian is someone possessed by the Holy Spirit and it is the same Holy Spirit for each Christian. It is not that each of us has a 'bit' of him but that he is present in each of us. How then can we avoid the conclusion that he must bring us together? Even the people who write the beer commercials for television have not missed this point. The drink brings you together and we are shown pictures of happy smiling, friendly faces having fellowship! To keep yourself to yourself is to parody the Christian experience. Look again at the words quoted above. 'Thinking and feeling alike . . . the same love . . . the same mind . . . a common care.' Could anything be more explicit? It makes me ashamed when I think of sections of the Church where these words are simply not true. Just as the beer commercials mislead us if we think we shall make satisfying friendships in any pub we happen to drop into, so the harsh unfriendliness of many a Christian group contradicts the promise of the 'fellowship of the Holy Spirit.' Yet it can be a reality and you have a vital part to play in allowing the Spirit to join you to others.

The same point is made in I Corinthians 12:13 where this sharing of the Holy Spirit is linked with Baptism.

In the same way, all of us, Jews and Gentiles, slaves and free men, have been baptised into the one body by the same Spirit, and we have all been given the one Spirit to drink.

Our very baptism is intended to remind us that Christianity is a corporate affair. Not aimlessly kicking a ball against a wall but a place in a team, where we can share with our fellow players and learn from them and the manager.

Let us look then at some of the practical implications of this truth that the Christian life is to be lived *corporately*.

COMMITTED TO THE LOCAL GROUP

A new Christian should first be committed to those who introduced him to Christ. For a young person who has just been confirmed this will mean commitment to his local church. But perhaps you found Christ in an office or a factory through the concern of a Christian friend. Or possibly you were converted at school or university through the Christian union. In each case, someone reached out to you in love. They prayed for you, talked to you and encouraged you. What is more natural than that you should love them in return by joining them in prayer and Christian witness? You should meet them regularly and talk and share with them. This 'meeting and talking' with other Christians is not something extra to loving

God and meeting him. It is one of the ways in which God meets and talks with you.

God is love, and whoever lives in love lives in God and God lives in him. The purpose of love being made perfect in us is that we may be full of courage on Judgment Day . . . because our life in this world is the same as Christ's.

I John 4:16, 17

COMMITTED TO THE LOCAL CHURCH

But you should not be content until you are also geared into a local church congregation. In this way you are drawn into a wider fellowship in which you not only meet other Christians from different jobs but where you can share in the wealth of Christian experience accumulated over hundreds of years. The most normal thing for a Christian to do is to be found among the worshipping people on a Sunday. I heard recently of a young man in the south-west of Uganda who walks twenty-five miles each Sunday in order to be 'in church.' That man is trying to be normal. The worship of the Church of England is summed up in the ancient phrase 'Word and Sacrament.' If we are to receive all that God wants to give us then we are to receive instruction from his Word; and we are to be strengthened in our faith by regular sharing in the Holy Communion.

But, it may be objected, why does our receiving 'Word and Sacrament' have to be done in a 'group' atmosphere? Surely it is enough if I, by myself, study the Bible and in my heart receive Christ? No, it is not enough, for the followng reasons.

THE WORD

The transmission of Christian truth through the centuries has depended on two activities of God. The first is the production and preservation of the Scriptures. Here is the rule of faith. In the Bible is contained what Jude called 'the faith which once and for all God has given to his people.' But it is also God's activity that this truth is passed from teacher to taught. So writes Paul to Timothy: 'Take the words that you heard me preach in the presence of many witnesses and give them into the keeping of men you can trust, men who will be able to teach others also.' Here then is living truth passed from one to another; truth in people. A 'new' Christian then should be able to come to his 'older' Christian teacher and hear the truth as the Bible is explained and expounded and see the truth in a life which is like Christ's.

Part of the new Christian's commitment to the Church is to come under instruction in an attitude of humility. As children approach maturity they tend to scorn and write off what their parents say. They would do better to respect the accumulated wisdom their parents have to offer. Of course parents can be wrong as can preachers and teachers but in the normal way the more experienced teach the less experienced. We do not expect to find an apprentice showing the master craftsman how to do it. The best preachers and teachers, in their turn, submit to the accumulated wisdom of the church as expressed in such outline statements as the ancient creeds. We do not think that, because we are modern, we are wiser than our fathers. That attitude can easily lead to unorthodoxy, error and disaster.

To many a young person this talk of 'being orthodox' may be like a red rag to a bull. Many are saying these days, 'The older generation has made such a mess of things, let us young ones with our new insights and enthusiasm come and make the Church what she ought to be. Or better still leave the stuffy old Church to stew in its juice and go and live in loving groups that are small enough to be real.' There is truth and error here. Yes, of course, often the Church is stuffy and hidebound and how much we need young people's freshness and willingness to experiment! But 'orthodox' means 'right belief' and it would be fatal to try to build your experiments on 'wrong belief.' I recently met some young people who had become involved in an unanchored Christian group that travels around doing evangelistic work. There was much to enjoy in Christian experience but the group was ruled in an authoritarian way which held the members in tyranny. I pointed out to these young people that Jesus and Peter had a very different style of leadership. We found it in the Bible and it was remarkable to see how the truth, when they read it, set them free. So read your Bible, soak yourself in God's truth – and if you must disagree with the doctrine of a more experienced Christian make sure you have massive grounds for doing so. It is so easy to be wrong and false doctrine quickly leads to shallow living and disillusioned experience.

THE SACRAMENTS

In all churches, it is obvious that the sacraments are something you do with other people. In the Church of England use, the sacraments are placed firmly in a 'group' context. Ideally, Baptism is administered when most of the local Christians are present. This then gives force to the welcoming of the candidate into God's family. The occasion is also a reminder to those present of their own Baptism and promises. The service is not just for spectators but one when the Church gathers to reaffirm its commitment to God and once more to take on its responsibility to bring up the newly baptised in the faith.

Similarly, the Prayer Book directs that Holy Communion cannot be celebrated by the Priest alone. It is not merely an act of private devotion but one where others must join him in worship. I find that coming to Communion gives an added depth to my awareness of Christ. It is like the difference between watching a film on television and seeing it in a full cinema. The large group of people, the wide screen, the concentrated attention, the audience reaction, the lack of distractions – all these give me a heightened enjoyment of the film and a closer look at what the film director is trying to say to me. Similarly I find that a well-filled church with everyone saying, for example, the Nicene Creed together gives me an assurance and strength that perhaps I cannot get in my personal devotions, important though they are.

JOINING A DENOMINATIONAL CHURCH

I suppose most people become a Christian through their local *church*. But I realise that many young people first find Christ in a school Christian society or in the university Christian union. However, the same principles apply. You have an obligation, a commitment to that group and you will find your fellowship among them as you receive instruction and take responsibility. But there is a difference: you must be realistic and look forward to the time when you leave. Where will your group commitment be then? It is very worrying that such a high proportion of young Christian people leaving their warm friendly Christian unions quickly drift away because they have no group anchors. Some Christians find faith in the factory or office group, but make little attempt to make links at home with the local Christian Church.

The best plan is to get well integrated with a mainstream denomination straight away. The particular kind of churchmanship you fell drawn to will depend on your temperament, your friends, your parents and the liveliness of the local specimens. But having made a reasonable choice (and see Chapter 7), stick to it! Remember it is a commitment. This may mean that when you move to another place the local church may not be as exciting as the one you are used to and it is tempting to search around for something more congenial. To do this is to miss the truth about the Church being 'catholic' that is, membership is open to all sorts. You must be willing to accept the cross-section of the Church. Not all your fellow-Christians will see eye to eye with you and none of them is perfect (but then neither are you, remember that!): but you are committed to love them and to worship with them. If you set out on a pilgrimage to find the Perfect Church you are bound to be disappointed and will finish up in a church with one member, you!

TAKING RESPONSIBILITY

It is interesting that in the New Testament, the word 'faithful' has a double meaning. In the first place it means someone who is *full of faith*, that is who believes in Christ. But such a man over the years becomes *faithful*, that is trustworthy. The man who relies on God becomes a man on whom God can rely, someone whom God can trust to go on doing things when it is difficult. Alfred Tucker was a man who put his faith in God and who was appointed to be Bishop of Eastern Equatorial Africa in place of the murdered Hannington. He went to Africa in 1890 and retired in 1911. In those years he *walked* 22,000 miles in evangelising and visiting young churches. There's faithfulness for you. In Matthew 25:21 the master in the parable says to his servant 'Well done good and *faithful* servant. You have been *faithful* in managing small amounts, so I will put you in charge of large amounts. Come on in and share my happiness!'

It will not be long, if you are committed to a group, before someone asks you to do something. It may be a very small job, like helping with the coffee, or it may be a very demanding job like teaching in the Sunday School. Your response should be glad and immediate: 'Of course I will help. I'd be delighted.' I know that sometimes we have to consider our studies, or the needs at home, but for a new Christian the instinctive reaction should be one of wanting to serve Christ in the group. Sometimes God wants to train us for bigger things by giving us small things at first; but sometimes a man's life commitment is made up of 'small things' – it is none the worse for that!

But whatever the case, like the violinist, you have a special part to play, a unique contribution to make. If you hold back, the group will be the poorer for it. The group is a body and if an arm or a toe is missing it will function inefficiently, even painfully. The leaders themselves are not always aware of this and if you should find that you have *not* been asked, first think and pray and then go and offer your services; they are not likely to be refused.

WHY SHOULD I BOTHER?

One can see then, both from the Bible and from experience, that the solitary Christian is a stunted Christian. But most of us are wilful and, in the first place, unwilling to submit to a group or have the inconvenience of a task that regularly claims our time, and we need to have good reasons why our commitment to Christ should inescapably lead to a commitment to the Church. Let me summarise them:

● It is commanded by Jesus himself. He told us to love each other.

● Jesus in his own life demonstrated his commitment to the group. He said that he was like a good shepherd willing to die for the sheep.

● To hold back from the fellowship is to deny that the Holy Spirit lives in us.

● To be loved by the group is to be valued, to be healed and made into a whole personality.

● You will be strengthened by the group especially in difficult times.

● The giving and receiving of love is the very business of being a Christian, being like God.

● The love of Christians for each other is one of the most effective ways of evangelism.

● You will have to live in a group in heaven, so you had better get used to it now!

Bible quotations for Chapter 2

AN UNLIKELY CONVERSATION

For he cannot love God, whom he has not seen, if he does not love his brother whom he has seen.   *I John 4:20*

And look out for each other's interests, not just for your own.   *Philippians 2:4*

And you have a sincere love for your fellow believers.   *I Peter 1:22*

A GROUP COMMITMENT

One flock with one shepherd.   *John 10:16*

I am the vine, you are the branches.   *John 15:5*

The family of God.   *Ephesians 2:19–22*

All of you then, are Christ's body, and each one is part of it. *I Corinthians 12:27*

FELLOWSHIP

. . . thankful for your partnership in the gospel from the first day until now.
                                                                 Philippians 1:5 (RSV)

. . . to share in his sufferings and become like him in his death.   *Philippians 3:10*

. . . any incentive of love, any participation in the Spirit . . . complete my joy by the same Spirit.   *Philippians 2:1, 2 (RSV)*

Let us be concerned with one another, to help one another to show love and to do good. Let us not give up the habit of meeting together, as some are doing.
                                                                 Hebrews 10:24, 25

COMMITTED TO THE LOCAL CHURCH

I felt the need of writing to you now to encourage you to fight on for the faith which once and for all God has given to his people.   *Jude 3*

Take the words that you heard me preach . . . and give them into the keeping of men you can trust.   *II Timothy 2:2*

Remember your former leaders, who spoke God's message to you. Think back on how they lived and imitate their faith.   *Hebrews 13:7*

Turn away from your sins, each one of you, and be baptised in the name of Jesus Christ.   *Acts 2:38*

This is my body which is for you. Do this in memory of me.   *I Corinthians 11:24*

COMMITTED TO THE WIDER CHURCH

The messengers were sent off and went to Antioch . . . where they gave them the letter. When the people read the letter they were filled with joy by the message of encouragement. Judas and Silas . . . spoke a long time with the brothers, giving them courage and strength. After spending some time there, they were sent off in peace . . .   *Acts 15:30–33*

TAKING RESPONSIBILITY

Well done good and faithful servant.   *Matthew 25:21*

Whoever shares what he has with others, must do it generously . . . Work hard and do not be lazy. Serve the Lord with a heart full of devotion.   *Romans 12:8, 11*

WHY SHOULD I BOTHER?

We are ruled by Christ's love for us.   *II Corinthians 5:14*

Questions for discussion

1 In what ways should you be joining in at your local church?
2 To whom do you owe a debt of love because they brought you to Christ? How could you return that love?
3 How do you fulfil your commitment to the wider Church?

3
A world commitment

The man without God tends to distract himself from life's large questions by filling every conscious moment with work or pleasure – people, books and films, eating, drinking, parties – in fact anything which will prevent him from asking where he is going to. Suppose that such a man becomes a Christian. To the onlooker, especially to the unbeliever, it would seem as though the man's horizons have drawn in. His life seems to have dwindled and he has become an unhealthy introvert. And, of course, if the new Christian remains in this state, continually bewailing his sins, preoccupied with his own failure, one could be excused for wondering if he has really tasted the freedom and peace that Christ offers to those who come to him.

But if the new Christian takes his decision seriously he soon begins to discover his group commitment and his life begins to expand, though this time in a more generous and God-like manner. For he finds that in Christ 'there is no difference between Jews and Gentiles, between slaves and free men, between men and women' (Galatians 3:28). He finds that in the Church he is forced into relationships with all sorts and so his life expands in a more varied way.

THE EXPANDING LIFE
Now this expansion will go still further. The Christian is not only committed to Christ and to the Church: he is committed to the whole world. And if this sounds rather grandiose for small insignificant me, I must realise that when I was first joined to Christ I was joining myself to the creator of all men, and so my interests are now

far wider than they were. It is a strange lie that has been circulat-
ing for centuries that Christians are those whose lives have con-
tracted, who are kill-joys and mere shades of their former, unin-
hibited selves. It is a lie, it must be confessed, that has found
support in the lives of some distorted Christians. But they are like
that, not because they are Christian but because they are not
Christian enough. The man who accepts the full implication of his
new relationship to God finds his life steadily expanding in richness
and interest. No doubt the sceptic may claim to be unable to see
this but the truth is to be found by the man who sees the Christian
life from the inside.

Before developing this idea of a 'world commitment,' it is necessary to distinguish between two senses of the word 'world' in the
New Testament. It is used in one sense in I John 2:15 ('Do not love
the world or anything that belongs to the world') where it means a
system opposed to God and his ways. In the bad sense of the word,
we have the world that crucified Christ. But there is another sense,
a neutral sense, in which it is used in passages like John 3:16 ('For
God loved the world so much that he gave his only Son . . .'). In
these passages 'world' is used to denote the whole of mankind. In
Chapter 6 I shall deal with some of the difficulties of living in the
'world' in the first sense. But here I wish to talk of world commitment in the second sense: the Christian is committed in love to all
men including those beyond the Christian family.

LOVE YOUR NEIGHBOUR

There are two sections of Jesus's teaching which illustrate the
nature of this world commitment. The first is the parable of the
Good Samaritan in Luke 10. The personal commitment has
already been spelled out by Jesus in the words of an Old Testament
quotation. 'You must love the Lord your God with all your heart,
and with all your soul, and with all your strength, and with all your
mind.' Then he indicates the wider implication, 'Love your neighbour!' In response to the cross-question he indicates what it means
to love your neighbour. He tells the story of a man who, coming
across someone in need of help, meets his need. The Samaritan
ignores racial prejudice, his own inconvenience and the cost. None
of these weigh with him at all. The narrative states with simplicity
'and when he saw the man his heart was filled with pity . . . and he
took care of him.' The contrast between this Samaritan and the

priest who passed by is shocking. The priest and the Levite did what came naturally and what the vast majority of men do every day. They ignored the battered man. If you had asked them two hours later what the man looked like they would have replied 'What man?'

God's requirement of us is that we should be neighbourly to all; to each man in need even if he isn't 'one of us.' For me it is clear teaching that my circle of caring must be drawn way beyond the Christian family. God is asking me to love the world. The parable of the sheep and the goats at the end of Matthew 25 makes it plain that I shall be judged at the last day by my attitude to Jesus and that this attitude will be monitored by God in my attitudes towards the needy, towards the world of my fellow men.

SPEAK THE WORD
The other section of Jesus's teaching is to be found right at the end of the gospels of Matthew and Mark and in Acts 1:8. 'Go then, to all peoples everywhere and make them my disciples.' Jesus sends us to the world, so that the world might hear his words and believe on him. When we speak of the Church as 'catholic,' we mean that membership is open to all. To believe this means in practice that we are committed to speak to the world, to whoever we can find to listen and to tell them that they have a place in Christ's Church if they will only turn to him in repentance and faith. You will hear it said, 'What you are speaks much louder than what you say' and of course it is true. If a man is not living a life of love like the Good Samaritan then it is no use his proclaiming a God of love in word. But some Christians draw quite a false conclusion from this truth. What they say, in effect, is this: 'I cannot bear the thought of being a hypocrite, someone who says one thing and does another. I know that often I fail to *live* as a Christian should, therefore I will not *speak* of Christ for fear of bringing his name into dishonour. I will proclaim Christ by what I *am* rather than by what I *say*.' This position may be sincerely held but it is false to the Christian commitment for these reasons:

● Jesus commands us to speak for him and failure to do so is disobedience. It is not 'either/or' word and action; it is 'both/and.'

● A *silent* Christian life can be positively misleading. Supposing a Christian in an office never mentions his allegiance to Christ and yet lives a fine upright life. Is he not providing ammunition for the observant humanist who says to himself 'There. It *is* possible to be a good man without being a Christian'?

● Christianity is *par excellence* the religion of the Word: God's definite and clear revelation of himself to man. How can the proper communication of this religion be in a silent word? How much better to do as Paul did and ask for his friends' prayers 'that I may be bold in speaking of the gospel, as I should' (Ephesians 6:20).

The Christian's world commitment thus may be expressed in two phrases: it is a ministry of Work and it is a ministry of Word. The word 'ministry' means 'service': we are called by God to serve not just our families, not just our Church-family, but the whole world and we are to bring to that world a Work of love and a Word of hope and rescue.

A WORK OF LOVE

A few years ago I was teaching the parable of the Good Samaritan to some young Africans in Uganda. I explained the meaning of the story which is (at least) that if you are travelling along a road and you find someone lying in it then you should pick him up. 'Ah, sir, but you don't understand our country. You should never stop, for thieves put decoys in the road and when you stop they will rob you.' I protested that a Christian would know how to trust God in such a situation but he dare not defy the plain teaching of Scripture. Two days later I was driving home in the dark about half past ten at night. And as I swept round a corner of the road my headlights picked out the body of a man lying in the road. Had I been going much faster I might have run over him. The test had come – and sooner than I thought! I stopped the car in the middle of the road about twenty yards away and waited with the engine switched off. No one in sight. 'Well,' I said to myself, 'can you trust God?' Leaving my wife in the car I made a gingerly approach, bent down and turned the man over. He was dead drunk so I started to drag him to the side of the road and almost immediately (they came from nowhere) I was surrounded by men! I couldn't speak the language, I couldn't explain that I hadn't knocked the man down. It turned out that the gathering crowd were locals and not robbers and I was allowed to drive off unmolested. I tell this story to illustrate how hard it is to do God's will. It is difficult when the instructions are as plain as can be: it can be even more difficult to find God's will in an ambiguous situation.

My real desire in that situation was to drive on. 'Don't get involved! It's nothing to do with you! Leave it till later when you can speak Luganda! Your wife is with you, it's not fair to expose her! . . .' And so on. We always have a hundred good reasons why we should not get involved. Some years ago in Bristol, I witnessed a street fight where a bully was beating up a weaker man. Did I get involved? No: I was scared stiff and gawped with the rest until I felt sick and turned away.

Now these two incidents I have mentioned were very obvious situations which demanded a Christian response. But where I and many of my brother Christians so often fail is that we do not get involved in the cases of need that we cannot see.

There are some we cannot see because they live far away. Where is this 'third world' they keep talking about? Well it's a long way away and we can't see it. It's true that some organisations like TEAR Fund or Oxfam keep pushing pictures of starving children in the papers. It is also true that journalists keep writing about disasters far away and the broadcasters show television pictures and give reports about human extremity in some forgotten corner. But by and large, we can pretend we don't see them. The whole philosophy of advertising has given us a semi-cynical approach to what is presented in the media: 'It probably isn't as bad as they make out.' What is certain is that you don't have to trip over the bodies when you walk down the street to the shops (where, incidentally, you can actually buy things). So, who is my neighbour? Where is this man in need?

Our generation has no excuse. One of the inferences of the communications revolution is that it has increased our guilt by giving us knowledge of those who need us. It is staggering that many of us in the Western world are struggling with a weight problem while two-thirds of the world is undernourished. Listen to John the Baptist, 'Whoever has two shirts must give one to the man who has none, and whoever has food must share it' (Luke 3:11). That's clear enough. What are we doing about it?

Then there are those we see with our eyes but we refuse to notice them. You may be aware that the children of some young mothers going out to work are being neglected. But what is being done to help them? How seriously does the Christian take the problems of local government, including housing? One Bishop of Rochester was passionately concerned about Road Safety. Often our world commitment is so weak we don't even challenge our friends about using safety belts. If we were injured in an accident we would be the first to be grateful for a pint of blood. It would probably come from a man who never goes to church. The rich man in the story in Luke 16 had a beggar in desperate trouble right at his gate, but he never saw him. Around us marriages are breaking down, babies are being unnecessarily aborted, family planning is not implemented, thousands are in mental hospitals who need compassion; alcoholics are desperate; discharged prisoners are bewildered. The Christian is committed to seeing these things. The works that Jesus did concerned the blind and the lame, the lepers and the deaf as well as the preaching of the gospel (Matthew 11:5).

We are often tempted to divide our lives into compartments and especially to keep the religious bit separate. A Christian with a true perspective, however, refuses to see his occupation merely as a job: he will see it as a vocation, a calling from God. In considering a career, a life's work, the new Christian should regard that job as part of his way of expressing his world commitment: it is not merely his way of earning a living. In some way every job ministers to human need and is God's way of meeting that need. This is true of accountants and farmers and tax inspectors just as much as of preachers and teachers. There may be some jobs, like running a betting shop, where the ministry is to the faulty side of human need and the Christian will avoid these. But a man making toys or emptying dustbins is committed to the world: the Christian difference is that he does it in obedience to and out of love for God.

A WORD OF HOPE

Let us move on from the works of practical love to the need to speak of Christ. I think it is important that Christian aid is given freely and generously, that God's work done in true love is aid 'without strings.' It is not Christian to go out to a man and say, in effect, 'I will give you a bowl of rice if you agree to become a Christian.' The whole point about love is that you simply care that the man is hungry. You are not trying to manipulate him. Of course, it is quite likely that if the man is touched by your pity then he may ask why you are doing it, but in the first place you care for him because he needs care. Having said that, no loving Christian should remain silent if he can possibly help it. God has sent him to speak a word after the pattern of Jesus: 'I gave them the message that you gave me, and they received it' (John 17:8); 'As the Father sent me, so I send you' (John 20:21).

The first point to emphasise is that 'Speaking Christianity' is not the preserve of only a few special Christians like preachers and broadcasters; it is the concern of *all* Christians. This is made clear by the word used by Jesus (recorded in Acts 1:8) that Christians are *witnesses*. This applied in the first place to the apostles who were witnesses in a special, unrepeatable way of the physical life, death and supernatural resurrection of the historical Jesus. But it is also true of Paul, who never knew Jesus 'in the flesh.' Ananias said to Paul, after his conversion, 'For you will be a witness for him to tell all men what you have seen and heard' (Acts 22:15).

Now *every* Christian has 'seen and heard' something. He has had some definite experience of God whether of forgiveness or peace or strength in temptation. And all he has to do, in order to be a witness, is to speak of what he has seen and heard. He does not have to do any study, he does not have to pretend. All he has to be is honest and willing. He may lay himself open to ridicule and he may find he is unable to answer the theological questions that people shoot at him in response. But he has been and is a witness and that is all he is required to be in the first instance. And I suppose more people have been drawn to Christ by a witness testifying than by an academic arguing because the truth of Christ has been displayed in a real, warm, human life and therefore is immediately seen to be relevant.

But sooner or later the Christian will be called on to give reasons for his faith, to give orthodox Christian views on the nature of God, on life after death, on the work of the Holy Spirit, to explain how it is that a good God allows evil in the world, to expound the Christian teaching on marriage and so on. So the new Christian who is prepared to witness will find himself driven to thought and prayer and study and will try to summarise the message which God has given to the world. For instance, from Mark 1:1–15 he may extract something like this:

●   All men should repent.
●   God's kingdom is very close because Jesus has come into the world.

● All men should believe the good news.
● Jesus wants men to be joined to him by the Holy Spirit.

Here is a message to be delivered, not distorted nor diluted. Under pressure from the world it is tempting to alter it but it is 'given' like the data in a problem. It is not our message; we are only the bearers of it for another.

In the Bible we have many stories of God's messengers and often we see that these people were reluctant to carry out their task. Moses was reluctant to deliver the message in Egypt because he was afraid of the danger. Jeremiah was reluctant because of his youth and inexperience. He was also, in later life, reluctant because he did not always agree with the message and he would have liked to have changed it. Hosea was reluctant because his life and unhappiness were part of the message. If you feel reluctant to take God's message to men I can assure you that you are not the first to feel like that and often for similar reasons. Paul in his letters is always asking for boldness in speaking the message which indicates that he frequently felt nervous and afraid when faced with worldly-wise men. Our feelings are not very important provided that we are obedient. What is disastrous is when we fail to deliver the message.

To sum up, then, the Christian's commitment is a world commitment. No part of the human race is in principle beyond his care. He may be called upon to go and live abroad to show care to those who are far away. He may be asked to give away half his income. He may enter 'the ministry' and so be a permanent full-time exhibit of Speaking Christianity. He may be a bus driver and be concerned about getting people to work on time and do it all as for God. But his commitment will be both of Work and Word and the reason is not far away. God himself, who is now joined to this Christian by the Holy Spirit, is a God of Work (does he not sustain everything?) and a God of the Word (has he not sent his Son to speak to us?). Of course *God* is committed to the world, so the Christian must bear the family likeness.

Bible quotations for Chapter 3

THE EXPANDING LIFE

(Jesus said,) I have come in order that they might have life, life in all its fulness.
John 10:10

May you be made strong with all the strength which comes from his glorious might, that you may be able to endure everything with patience. *Colossians 1:11*

LOVE YOUR NEIGHBOUR

Love your neighbour as yourself. *Mark 12:31*

Share your belongings with your needy brothers, and open your homes to strangers. *Romans 12:13*

To love, then, is to obey the whole Law. *Romans 13:10*

SPEAK THE WORD

You will be filled with power when the Holy Spirit comes on you and you will be witnesses for me. *Acts 1:8*

How can they hear, if the message is not proclaimed? And how can the message be proclaimed, if the messengers are not sent out? *Romans 10:14, 15*

They were all filled with the Holy Spirit and began to speak God's message with boldness. *Acts 4:31*

A WORK OF LOVE

This is what God the Father considers to be pure and genuine religion: to take care of orphans and widows in their suffering, and to keep oneself from being corrupted by the world. *James 1:27*

Suppose there are brothers or sisters who need clothes and don't have enough to eat. What good is there in saying to them, 'God bless you! Keep warm and eat well!' – if you don't give them the necessities of life? *James 2:15, 16*

Questions for discussion

1 How far is it true to say that Christians live very constricted lives?

2 Should Christians be involved in relief organisations which are Christian (lie TEAR Fund, Christian Aid) or organisations which are neutral (like Oxfam, National Society for the Prevention of Cruelty to Children)?

3 What are the main reasons for a new Christian being unwilling to speak about Jesus to his friends?

4
Law and grace

In the first three chapters I outlined the nature of the Christian commitment. In these next three chapters I am going to consider the same three relationships (with God, with the Church, with the world) in another way in an attempt to get to the heart of the Christian difference of attitude.

TWO KINDS OF RELATIONSHIP

First of all I wish to contrast two kinds of relationships which occur among human beings. The first situation is where one man is employed by another. The hours are agreed, the wages are fixed and the work is outlined. From the first day the employer expects as his right that the employee will do his work regularly and conscientiously. Conversely, the employee will expect as his right that at the end of the week he will be paid. A contract might be drawn up, but even if it is not, the rights of the two parties are safeguarded by common law and statute. And if things go wrong the aggrieved party can take the other to court and insist under the law that his rights are enforced. If you asked the worker on Friday, 'Will you get paid tonight?' he could reply, 'Oh yes. You see I've put in my hours and worked efficiently and therefore I confidently expect my wages. And if I don't get them there'll be trouble!' If the worker should eventually leave the employment then the final pay-packet will discharge the employer's duties and the relationship is at an end.

In the second situation also, money changes hands but the two parties are now a man and his nephew. On the nephew's 20th birthday his uncle tells him that he wants to give him £500 when he is 21. There is no particular reason why the uncle should do this; it is just that he is fond of the boy. The young man has not been expecting the gift. He has done nothing to earn it, indeed if he had done then it would not be a gift but a reward. Nor does the uncle expect any services from his nephew once the gift has been made; if he does, then it is not a gift but a bribe or an inducement or wages in advance. The recipient of the gift has no right to receive it. If you asked him, 'Will you get your money?' he might reply, 'Oh yes I'm sure I will. You see, uncle is not only rich: he's extremely honest and reliable. I know he wouldn't break his word. I trust him implicitly.' In due course the 21st birthday arrives and the gift is made. Far from ending the relationship the handing over of the money deepens it and the two men grow in love towards each other.

PERSONAL AND IMPERSONAL
These two kinds of relationship have quite a different feel to them. The relationship between the uncle and his nephew is intensely personal and loving: there is no sense of bargaining or counting the cost. The money that changes hands is a symbol of something deep and important: it is not a value which somehow measures affection. If the uncle did not make the gift it would be quite inappropriate to talk of taking him to court. Even if such an action were possible and successful it would completely fail to restore a personal rift between the two men.

In the case of the other relationship, the matter is far more impersonal, especially if the employer is the state or a very large business. The employee is looked upon as a source of work or a unit of cost while the employer is seen just as a large machine which produces the wage-packet in response to a correctly stamped time-card. The relationship is carefully controlled by a set of rules and if something goes wrong it can be taken to arbitration where the rights of the two parties can be weighed up against each other.

I am going to style these two kinds of relationships as personal and impersonal. I appreciate that employment relationships can be very personal and friendly just as some family relationships can be all to do with money. But this is because our relationships are complex and the impersonal pure and simple is found to be unsatisfying. However the basic question which I want to raise is this: if God has dealings with man, are those dealings personal or impersonal? Is the relationship a kind of deal with rights and duties, work and reward? Or, is it based on promise, love and gratitude? Is the relationship an arrangement which might be ended by either party or is it permanent?

The answer to this question is of great importance for my dealings with God will affect my dealings with others, that is to say, my whole life. If I am not clear about the basis of my attitudes, I shall probably get the whole thing wrong.

THE ESSENTIAL GOSPEL

Now St Paul notices this distinction between personal and impersonal religion though he does not actually use those terms. He says in Romans 4:4:

A man who works is paid; his wages are not regarded as a gift but as something that he has earned.

Paul also notices that the strict Jew tends to regard his relationship to God in impersonal terms:

You call yourself a Jew; you depend on the Law and boast about God; you know what God wants you to do, and you have learned from the Law to do what is right. *Romans 2:17, 18*

In other words the Jew says, 'I have my part to play, to keep the Law. If I do this, then God will save me and welcome me and make me his own. Moses declared God's side that he would bless Israel and for our part we will keep God's commandments. If we do so, we shall be right to congratulate ourselves.' Paul challenges this whole notion of an impersonal relationship whereby we can work hard and somehow satisfy God's demands. He says that whatever we receive from God must be as a gift and that our relationship with him is thus rooted in love:

For it is by God's grace that you have been saved, through faith. It is not your own doing, but God's gift. There is nothing here to boast of, since it is not the result of your own efforts. *Ephesians 2:8, 9*

But God has shown us how much he loves us: it was while we were still sinners that Christ died for us. *Romans 5:8*

Please note that Paul is not making a mere suggestion. His teaching, he claims, is revealed to him by God: it is the essential gospel revealed by Jesus Christ to him as an apostle. God's relationship with man is not and never can be impersonal: man cannot earn a place in heaven. The true gospel is that God loves us and sent Christ to die for us, to deal with sin, that his sending of Christ is a free gift which can be ours simply by receiving it.

Now you may be tempted to say 'Does it make all that much difference?'

Perhaps already in this chapter you have begun to get tired of all this serious talk and feel that I am theorising too much. Let me remind you of the importance of truth. Truth or the lack of it is the basis of our living and if you have not understood the basic nature of the Christian religion, you will never be at heart a Christian and neither will your attitudes be Christian. Paul is a vivid demonstration of this. He was brought up as a strict follower of the Law; he was a proud Pharisee; so he hated the name of Jesus and he persecuted to the death the people who followed the way of Jesus. He was then brought to face the truth. He was brought to realise his pride, his sin and his cruelty. He discovered that his impersonal religion did not put him right with God. He was confronted by the living Jesus and was called to repentance. He then entered into a personal relationship with God through the Holy Spirit and he was a changed man! No wonder Paul got excited and angry when the early Galatian Christians began to replace their personal relationship to God with a set of impersonal rules.

You will never have that 'Christian Difference' that Paul had unless you understand the *personal* nature of your relationship to God. God saves you not by Law, but by grace through faith. Let me briefly expand these three ideas.

NOT BY LAW

Paul spent the first half of his life devoted to the Law of God found in the Old Testament, learning it and trying to keep it. The experience did not bring him peace for he found that however well he did there was always some point in which he was failing. He found that the Law was his accuser:

I would not have known what it is to covet if the Law had not said 'Do not covet.'
Romans 7:7

So Paul argues this out:

● The Law of the Old Covenant is good and might well bring life but as a matter of fact no one has come anywhere near keeping it completely.

● Because the Law was spoken by God it means that the whole human race is judged by the Law and found guilty. This means that every person is under God's judgment.

● This is frightening, for no one can hide and no one can escape. In due course every one of us must come before God's judgment seat. His justice is perfect which means that no one can be let off.

● On that Judgment Day we shall have to say something. But what could we say to justify ourselves? God knows everything and he knows we have all broken the Law.

● It follows that religion based on Law and human effort is totally ineffective, because an appeal to the Law can only be to your greater condemnation.

Ask the average man what his idea is about being Christian and he may say something like this, 'Well I think that God writes down all the good things we do and all the bad things we do and we hope that in the end the thing will balance up and with luck we may come out on the right side.' This view is certainly not Christian. In the first place if you have done a bad deed like being cruel to Jones, it is difficult to see how giving money to Smith could 'cancel out' the hurt to Jones. And in the second place it would mean that if by 'being a good chap' you could earn God's favour, then you would be able to boast in his presence and treat him as a kind of equal. You would be claiming your 'rights.' But because of the Law it is clear that if you had your 'rights' then you would be condemned for spoiling God's creation.

BUT BY GRACE

But God loves us even though we do not deserve it, and that is what the word 'grace' means. A parent shows he loves his child not because of the fame or the money it may bring, but because he loves the child for its own sake. Sometimes children behave in a cruel or thoughtless fashion towards the parents but it does not destroy the love they get.

The gospel is a matter of grace – that is, it springs entirely from God's side because he loves us even if we are unlovable. And even though we behave badly his love does not grow less. This truth is of great comfort to the Christian. It does not matter who you are or what you have done; God loves you without wavering and continues to offer his best gifts. Believe this and you are saved. The contrast between the true personal Christian gospel and impersonal religion is bluntly stated in Romans 6:23:

For sin pays its wage – death; but God's free gift is eternal life in union with Christ Jesus our Lord.

However we must not gloss over the real and deep spiritual difficulty that is raised by holding these two statements as true:

● Every man is condemned by God's Law, because every man has sinned.
● Every man is welcomed by God's love because God 'wants all men to be saved.'

How is it possible for God's Law to be upheld without condemning all men? Can God forgive the sinner without making light of sin?

The Christian answer, especially as explained by Paul, is that the death of Christ in our place meets the demand of the Law, so that a man may, if he wish, go free and be forgiven. There is no dilution of the seriousness of sin. Sin is serious all right, as we see that it killed Jesus. But God dealt with sin on the cross of Jesus and his action is a gift to us. We could not possibly earn it or work for it because all that man does is tainted by sin and pride. But the sinless Jesus could and did do a work on our behalf.[1]

The main point I am making here, however, is that the centre of the gospel is a gift, a promise made to you by God. He does this in love and grace. You do not have to try and 'get into God's good books.' Your response to God's offer must be personal rather than impersonal. Supposing, from the example given at the beginning of this chapter, that the nephew on hearing his uncle's promise said, 'In that case I will come and spend every Saturday tidying your garden,' the exasperated reply might well be, 'But I don't *want* you to come every Saturday. This is a gift, not wages!' Of course the uncle would like to see more of his nephew but he does not want it to seem that their relationship depends on a kind of bargain. It depends on love.

THROUGH FAITH

Your response to God, therefore, should be one of personal love. This is seen in two ways. First a real repentance when you admit how much you have grieved him and made him unhappy. To love

God in this way is to try to imagine how he feels to see his creation spoiled and his image in man defaced and distorted. Secondly, a grateful 'thank you' to God for his gifts: his gift of Christ and his gift of the Holy Spirit. The only thing that you contribute is the empty hand of the grateful receiver. This 'empty hand' is faith. You have to believe, for the offer has been made in the form of a promise.

If you have to go away from home and have been offered a bed for the night then all you have to do during the day is simply to believe it. Believing means not booking a room at an hotel, and then just turning up to claim the promise.

This is what you must believe as a true Christian:

●   That God really does love you.
●   That God provided the complete means for your forgiveness when Jesus died on the cross.
●   That God has promised you a full and satisfying life.
●   That God will give you himself in the person of the Holy Spirit.

If you truly believe this, then God actually joins himself to you and you become a Man-in-Christ. And as this new life develops it is better to describe it by saying you *believe in* God, than to say you *believe that* God loves you. It is a real trust *in* him rather than a theoretical belief *about* him.

It is of course the gift of the Holy Spirit that underlines my main point in this chapter that God's dealings with us are *personal* rather than *impersonal*. For the Holy Spirit is God *in person*. The Bible never speaks of the Holy Spirit as 'it' but always as 'he.' It is wrong to think of him as a kind of 'force,' like electricity.

When the gospel came to Samaria (the story is in Acts 8) Simon, the Great Power, 'believed' (v13). Then 'he offered money to Peter and John and said, "Give this power to me too, so that anyone I place my hands on will receive the Holy Spirit." But Peter answered him "May you and your money go to hell, for thinking you can buy God's gift with money! . . . your heart is not right." ' (vv 18–21) Simon's mistake was that he believed in impersonal religion. He thought he could handle God and use him for himself: he missed the point badly. God the Holy Spirit is a person and cannot be bought and sold. And all deep dealings with God must be personal, with man always in debt to God.

THE KEY WORDS
To summarise so far it will be helpful to pick out the key words in these two different kinds of relationships:

IMPERSONAL COMMITMENT (LIKE EMPLOYER–EMPLOYEE)
Work, wages, rights, law, self-reliance, justice. The contract can be ended with both parties satisfied.

PERSONAL COMMITMENT (LIKE UNCLE–NEPHEW)
Love, grace, gift, promise, faith, gratitude, humility, forgiveness. The 'contract' is permanent and always capable of enrichment.

The one true gospel is a story of God's *personal* offer to man. This truth needs holding on to. You must grab it with both hands and resist all temptation to have it pulled away. The temptation is to legalise the gospel, that is to reduce Christianity to a set of rules. Few groups of Christians have been more concerned about the preaching of the gospel than the Plymouth Brethren. Yet certain of their assemblies have become 'closed' through the legalising of the gospel. The East African revival has had great influence and brought hundreds of thousands into personal Christianity. Yet there have arisen among these people those who have tried to give certain rules to ensure purity of living. No church has a better biblical basis than the Church of England and yet there is a large number of Anglicans who think that Christianity is merely 'going to church and trying to do your best.'

Here are four pieces of history to underline what I am saying:

*THE CONFLICT BETWEEN JESUS
AND THE PHARISEES*
Why did the Pharisees dislike Jesus so much and how is it that Jesus's strongest words are spoken against them? Luke 15 indicates the answer. The chapter begins with the Pharisees grumbling at the grace of Jesus in eating with 'outcasts' and three parables are then told which are directed against the Pharisees. In the first two they are indirectly accused of failing to rejoice over a repentant sinner but in the third the older son (15:25–32) is clearly meant to be a picture of those who claim to be doing God's will but whose attitudes are far from his. First, the older son was angry because of his father's generosity and secondly (v30) he despised his brother

because he regarded himself as blameless. This dislike of grace and insistence on self-righteousness show the Pharisees' theological position.

In 18:9–14 Luke points out the purpose of the parable of the Pharisee and the tax collector. 'Jesus told this parable to people who were sure of their own goodness and despised everybody else.' The Pharisees' approach to God was legalistic, *ie* based on Law. They thought they were approved by keeping the rules. 'Hypocrites!' said Jesus. 'You give to God one tenth even of the seasoning herbs . . . but you neglect the really important teachings of the law, such as justice and mercy and honesty . . . inside you are full of violence and selfishness' (Matthew 23:23, 25). Their whole thinking was foreign to the personal gospel.

THE CONTROVERSY OF ACTS 15

The first major theological disagreement in the New Testament Church was about the impersonal gospel. Some of the believers who belonged to the party of the Pharisees said of the newly-converted Gentiles: 'They have to be circumcised and told to obey the Law of Moses.' It is not difficult to understand why they said this. All the first Christians were Jews and they continued to be practising Jews after their conversion to Christ. After all they had not started to believe in a new God. They still worshipped the God of the Old Testament though now they perceived that he is indeed 'the Father of our Lord Jesus Christ.' The Old Testament scriptures were not abandoned: rather they continued to keep the Law of Moses and to circumcise their male babies. All this is natural enough and in Acts 21 we find even Paul preparing to keep the Passover in the Temple and to submit to the Jewish ceremony of purification.

But the difficulty arises over *Gentile* converts. According to the story of Acts 10 and 11 it seems at first that the Christian leaders were reluctant to think that it was possible for Gentiles to receive the Holy Spirit at all. But events convinced them. Then followed a period of expansion among the Gentiles pioneered by Paul but centred on Antioch rather than Jerusalem. Should the new Gentile Christians be asked to submit to the Law? Peter's answer in 15:10, 11 is the key to the question, 'We believe and are saved by the grace of the Lord Jesus, just as they are.' Note the two 'personal' words, 'faith' and 'grace.' The decision was that a legalistic requirement should *not* be placed on the Gentile Christians but that they should be asked in love to abstain from certain things that would give offence to their brother Jewish Christians.

It was a near thing. Had that decision gone the other way Christianity would have become merely a Jewish Sect and the glorious personal gospel would have been lost for ever. Paul realised this and hence his violent and almost abusive opening of his letter to the Galatians: a short pungent epistle devoted to one end, to maintain the one true gospel.

THE RISE OF ISLAM

The religion of Islam seems to me to be the next stage in this struggle. The Church having been founded on the truth of the gracious gospel, there appears in the Eastern Mediterranean a strong, simply expressed impersonal religion. It came in the seventh century and swept all before it especially in North Africa. The Way of Salvation in Islam is based on Five Pillars:

1 Recital of a one line creed that God exists and Mohammed is his prophet
2 The saying of prayers
3 Annual fasting
4 Giving alms
5 Pilgrimage to Mecca

Do these things and you will live; you will be acceptable to Allah. Note especially the simplicity of the demands which could, with effort, be kept. Nothing as penetrating as the Ten Commandments (especially the tenth!). Note too that there is nothing of what God offers, only of Man's duties.

Here is a basic question to ask all the other religions when you wonder if it is possible for Christianity alone to be right: is it a personal or an impersonal religion? No other religion that I have come across can offer, as a gift, the riches of Christ, found in the Holy Spirit.

THE STATE OF THE CHURCH
LEADING TO THE REFORMATION

Although in many places the Church was overwhelmed by the Islamic warriors, the gospel was not extinguished. The next danger came from within, a theology of justification by works. Some of the worst evidences of this theology of the Church in the sixteenth century were the buying of Masses, the sale of indulgences and false doctrines of penance. The underlying theology was that the Church was the custodian of salvation and could dispense grace and salvation in return for money or appropriate degrading acts.

It was Martin Luther, in 1515 while he was meditating on Paul's letter to the Romans, who wrote these words:

Night and day I pondered until I saw the connection between the justice of God and the statement that 'the just shall live by his faith.' Then I grasped that the justice of God is that righteousness by which through grace and sheer mercy God justifies us through faith. Thereupon I felt myself to be reborn. . . . The whole of Scripture took on a new meaning. . . . If you have a true faith that Christ is your Saviour, then at once you have a gracious God, for faith leads you in and opens up God's heart and will, that you should see pure grace and overflowing love.

You can hear the key words of the personal gospel ringing out: grace, faith, gracious, love. This teaching of Luther's was no new teaching. He had, under God's illumination, stripped away the legalistic shroud that was enveloping the Church.

PRACTICAL IMPLICATIONS OF THE ONE GOSPEL

Let us learn from history the true nature of God and his gospel. Let us hold on to God's grace. If I do then I will become 'different.' Here are some of the 'differences':

● I will become a humble person. Anyone who has been honoured far beyond what he deserves is bound to become humble and grateful. There will be no self-righteousness in the man who knows that only God can approve and acquit.

● I will be reluctant to despise others. If all men are fellow-sinners who am I to point the finger? In my capacity as a school teacher, I may be required to provide sober estimates of people. But what I produce will never be done with a sense of superiority.

● I will be grateful for what God gives me, not only in matters of 'salvation' but in practical things like money, a house, a job. Grateful and therefore content: not always striving for self-advancement.

● I will become a student of God's promises. I shall wish to increase my faith by knowing more of what God offers. I must study and then put my new found facts to the test; trusting God for all that he can do for me and for those things I long for.

And all this is very different from what I am by nature. It is easy to see why the Pharisees *hated* Jesus. They were proud; they despised others; they wanted more money; they only looked for rules. So when Jesus started to state the exact opposite then they knew that if they listened to him they would have to change – and they couldn't face it. But the offence of the gospel is that we are all Pharisees underneath. We would prefer a list of rules; we would like a simple fivefold path; we would like to be able to discharge our duty to God with money.

The warning is direct: men change very slowly and many Christians are reluctant to change in their hearts and accept God's grace as a gift. One of the greatest temptations you will face as a new Christian is to reduce Christianity to a set of rules or worse still to accept without question, from older Christians, a fixed pattern of life regarded as respectable. Such a life may be approved by men but are you sure it is approved by God? I would love to give you a long list of 'do's' and 'don'ts' and say, 'Here, keep this and you'll be a good Christian.' And no doubt you would like me to do so. What is required is much more laborious and painful. It is that you should be the humble, grateful recipient of God's grace and daily search his promises to find out which way he is leading you.

NOTE

1 This death of Christ is the very basis of the Christian's relationship to God and it is important that you should study it carefully. The New Testament passages which are particularly helpful are Mark 10:35–45; Romans 1–7; Galatians 1:11–3:29; Hebrews 5–10. But to get the most out of it you will probably need the help of a book, *eg The Work of Christ* by I. Howard Marshall (Paternoster).

Bible quotations for Chapter 4

THE ESSENTIAL GOSPEL

For it is by God's grace that you have been saved, through faith. It is not your own doing, but God's gift. There is nothing here to boast of, since it is not the result of your own efforts. *Ephesians 2:8, 9*

(Paul said,) 'I received strict instruction in the Law of our ancestors. . . . I persecuted to the death the people who followed this Way (*ie* Christians). As I was travelling, a bright light flashed from the sky . . . and I heard a voice saying . . . 'Why do you persecute me?' *Acts 22:3, 4, 6, 7*

But God was merciful to me, because I did not believe and so did not know what I was doing. And our Lord poured out his abundant grace on me and gave me the faith and love which are ours in union with Christ Jesus. *I Timothy 1:13, 14*

I am surprised at you! In no time at all you are deserting the one who called you by the grace of Christ, and are going to another gospel. *Galatians 1:6*

NOT BY LAW

God's wrath is revealed coming down from heaven upon all the sin and evil of men, whose evil ways prevent the truth from being known. *Romans 1:18*

It was not because of any good works that we ourselves had done, but because of his own mercy . . . the Holy Spirit gives us new birth and new life. *Titus 3:5*

BUT BY GRACE

Because of his own mercy . . . he saved us through the washing by which the Holy Spirit gives us new birth and new life. For God abundantly poured out the Holy Spirit on us, through Jesus Christ our Saviour, that by his grace we might be made right with God and come into possession of the eternal life we hope for. This is a true saying. *Titus 3:5–7*

THROUGH FAITH

I tell you the truth: whoever hears my words, and believes in him who sent me, has eternal life. *John 5:24*

In this way God shows that he himself is righteous and that he puts right everyone who believes in Jesus. *Romans 3:26*

WHAT YOU MUST BELIEVE

THE LOVE OF GOD

This is how God showed his love for us: he sent his only Son into the world that we might have life through him. *I John 4:9*

THE CROSS OF JESUS

This is what love is: it is not that we have loved God but that he loved us and sent his Son to be the means by which our sins are forgiven. *I John 4:10*

GOD PROMISES SALVATION
(A FULL AND SATISFYING LIFE)
Christ Jesus came into the world to save sinners.   *I Timothy 1:15*

THE PROMISE OF THE HOLY SPIRIT
... the Father in heaven will give the Holy Spirit to those who ask him!
Luke 11:13

PRACTICAL IMPLICATIONS OF THE ONE GOSPEL

God resists the proud, but gives grace to the humble.   *I Peter 5:5*

Do not judge others, so that God will not judge you.   *Matthew 7:1*

How great is the joy I have in my life in the Lord!   *Philippians 4:10*

In this way he has given us the very great and precious gifts he promised, so that by means of these gifts you may ... come to share the divine nature. *II Peter 1:4*

A WARNING

Keep watch over yourselves ... the time will come when some men from your own group will tell lies to lead the believers away after them. Watch, then ...
Acts 20:28, 30, 31

Questions for discussion

1   What does it mean to be 'justified by faith'? Why is it wrong to try to be 'justified by works'?
2   If the Law cannot save us, does this mean that Christians do not have to try to keep the Ten Commandments?
3   If God has given so much to us, what does this imply as to how we should give?

5
Expecting nothing in return

Suppose we climbed into our time-machine and arrived at Lyons say in the middle of the second century A.D. How much would we be able to identify? We would spot the Roman soldiers because of their armour and we would have little difficulty in identifying the rich merchants because of their houses and the way they dressed. But how would you identify the Christians? Here is a man who might be one, but he does not have a Bible because books are scarce, so it is no good asking if he takes daily Bible reading notes. On the first day of the week he goes to a breaking of bread with others but very early so that he can get off to his work on time. So many of the features of his daily life are different from our culture, what do we look for in his behaviour different from others to convince us that he really is a Christian?

The difference I would look for is that special attitude which is only found in those who are related to God in gift and gratitude. This attitude is God-like and can be summed up in these words 'expecting nothing in return.' For this is the way God loves us; this is another way of talking about grace. God is open towards us even though we are often closed towards him. God the creator is continually open towards men otherwise they would cease to exist instantly. Yet men still reject him while God still hopes for their response. He goes on hoping because he loves them; what he does not do is to stand on his rights and say, 'You *must* respond to me.' This marvellous way God has is to be the mark of the Christian; he is to show a likeness of being open-ended in love.

Do good, and lend, expecting nothing in return; and your reward will be great, and you will be sons of the Most High; for he is kind to the ungrateful and the selfish.   *Luke 6:35 (RSV)*

This 'openness' is found only in the man who believes he is saved by grace through faith. It is not that a man first believes the doctrine and then becomes open. It is that his becoming open is an embodiment of his belief. For the great truth of 'faith only' is what makes a man truly humble in love and this is why we find him 'expecting nothing in return.'

What I am going to do is to show how the truths in Chapter 4 when taken deeply into man's mind will fashion his behaviour towards others and make him like God. We forgive others, because we have been forgiven. We tell the truth because God tells the truth. We keep our promises because our health depends on God keeping his promises. And we love our enemies because Christ loved his enemies even while they were murdering him. I am not falling into the trap I warned you of in the last chapter; making a set of rules. . . . Thou shalt forgive others *etc*. I am saying we should become like God in his character, forgiving, truthful, reliable, open. For if I have opened my life to his life then it is inevitable that his life will flow into mine and that others should then be able to see God's life in me. I will be 'different' and it will be the 'difference' of God himself.

FORGIVING OTHERS

Let us start by looking at Jesus's story about the unforgiving servant in Matthew 18. A servant owed his King 'millions of pounds' and when he pleaded for time to pay, to his astonishment the King wrote off the whole debt and told him to forget it. Now if the King had sued for his rights under law the man would have had to try and repay it, say at £10 a week for 2000 years. Clearly this would be impossible. So the King in his mercy moved the whole relationship out of 'Law' into 'grace' and forgave him the whole debt. The servant went straight out and grabbed a man who owed him 'a few pounds' and when he in his turn begged for clemency he was refused and was thrown into jail. It is important to notice that the man who committed him to jail was within his rights. What' is horrifying is that he had received so much under 'grace' and yet when it suited him he tried to get more under 'Law.' We are not surprised at the King's reaction: 'You should have had mercy on your fellow servant, just as I had mercy on you.'

The application of the story is blindingly obvious. We have been forgiven so many sins by God we should be eager and willing to forgive the relatively few sins that have been committed against us by men. One of the effects of the remission of that enormous debt should have been to make the servant like his master, to make him gracious, and it would have done if he had been genuinely grateful. But he was not grateful. One can only imagine him coming away from that interview, congratulating himself on his good luck and determined to cash in on it. Not a thought for the kindness and love of his King and therefore not a spark of love in his own heart. Had that spark been there he would have responded instantly in mercy to his fellow servant who asked for it. But there was nothing in him but self-regard, what the forgiveness would mean to him: not a glance over the shoulder as to what it had *cost* the King to release him from his indebtedness!

Suppose that somebody has wronged you. Let us say that you have secured a promise from them to help in the preparation for a party and then at the last minute they let you down and you have to rush round in order to fill the gap. What is your immediate attitude to that person? 'Well, that's the last time I ask *him* to do anything'; in other words you are starting to break up the friendship. Now this will not do. You are a Christian and have tasted the grace of God. *He* has been open to you; will *you* now be closed to your friend? What should your attitude be? Perhaps something like this:

● Am I to blame at all for the other person not keeping his promise? Did I make it quite clear as to how soon the party was? Or how much work was involved? If I am at all to blame I had better apologise.

● Have I let down anyone in a similar way recently? No, of course not! But wait a minute what about . . .? Oh! that was different! You see, I had to . . . Had to? Well, perhaps it was a bit mean. . . . (For a start then, you know yourself to be not wholly blameless.)

● The person who has wronged you turns up to say sorry. What a relief! It means that God is going to put it right. In gratitude you accept the apology: 'That's all right!' and it really is all right and you proceed to forget it in the same way that God has forgotten your sins.

● Your friendship with the other person is deepened and there is more love than before. And you know there is a fund of goodwill on the other side if at a later date *you* should wrong *him*. This makes your life more secure because as time goes on you can rely on the goodwill of more and more people. If this sounds selfish I can only say that God's way will always turn out to be the best in the end for everyone and that includes you.

The Christian, then, has a headstart on the others when it comes to making relationships: he has learnt to say 'sorry,' in the first place to God, and then to other people. In his gratitude he becomes gracious and is able to bear injuries done to him and to offer forgiveness to those who ask for it.

TELLING THE TRUTH

The whole of the Christian's hope is built on a belief that Jesus and Peter and Paul and John and the rest are telling the truth. If they are not then we are indeed lost and they are the blind leaders of the blind. They insist however that they *are* telling the truth.

JESUS: I am the truth.   *John 14:6*
PETER: I am a witness of Christ's sufferings.   *I Peter 5:1*
PAUL: What I write is true. I am not lying, so help me God!
                                                                       Galatians 1:20
JOHN: *(he writes of himself as 'he')* He is the disciple who spoke of these things . . . and we know that what he said is true.
                                                                        John 21:24

How grateful we are to them, for a distortion would have been fatal to the message. We could never be sure of what God had said or even if he had spoken at all.

How important then for Christians, whose very existence depends on the truth being told, to be those who can be relied on to tell the truth. 'No more lying, then! Everyone must tell the truth to his brother, because we are all members together in the body of Christ' (Ephesians 4:25).

It is very easy to tell lies: small ones, big ones, white ones and partial ones. The most common is the lie which covers up some other wrong doing. Faced with an accusation, even caught in the act, we lie subtly or blatantly in an attempt to avoid the evil consequences of our misdeeds. Six years of school teaching has shown me how expertly and instantaneously people will lie to avoid trouble. But when they leave school they do not leave lying behind as they mature in other directions. 'Watergate' will, I suppose, pass into the English language for all time to stand for 'cover up.' Some of the culprits in that affair have appeared as overgrown schoolboys willing to say anything to excuse themselves. But the truth is deeper than that: it is that *all* men and women, five years old and fifty-five years old, will tell lies to avoid difficulties. The Christian should not have to 'cover up.' After all he is used to everything being open to God: he can afford to be open with others.

What about 'white lies'? We don't like hurting other people's feelings, so surely it is sometimes permissible? Very occasionally I think it can be correct to say that love demands a lie. But these cases are very few and far between. What we forget is that people will be hurt far less by the truth than by a genial, social, smoothing-over remark. Of course we are not to be brash and rude in speaking the truth but a genuine honest statement can be health-giving. We all know how a proud, selfish man can be a pain in the neck to all around him. Have you ever considered telling him so? It's a daunting prospect! But how will he come to repentance without the truth?

And then, the boasting lies. Often small, a little exaggeration here and there (storyteller's 25% licence) and it makes a bad story a good one and a good story hilarious. 'So I said to this chap, "You nefarious old goat. You should look where you're going." ' In fact you were rather frightened of him and said nothing of the sort. This is stupid, unthinking boasting and it fools no one. This is not the way a gracious man talks; the man whose whole life, down to the last second, is known to God, the God of truth.

KEEPING YOUR PROMISES

The Christian's cosmic destiny depends on whether or not God keeps his promise. If you say to me, 'Are you going to heaven? Where will you be on Judgment Day?' I must reply, 'It all depends on God's promise.' In Romans 4 Paul points out that it has always been this way. Long before the Law was given to Moses, Abraham had to depend on God's promise and so he is the father of all who have faith. God's grace is promised to me ('I will never turn away anyone who comes to me,' said Jesus in John 6:37) and if he doesn't keep his promise I have no assurance of anything at all.

It is true that sometimes we cannot keep our promises due to circumstances beyond our control. On your way to an appointment you might be taken ill. But usually fulfilment depends not on our being prevented but on our good will or lack of it. C. S. Lewis and his friend Paddy Moore promised each other that if anything happened in the First World War then each would care for the other's family. Moore was killed and Lewis gave Mrs Moore a home until 1951. That is promise-keeping. And do not think that when a promise is relatively trivial (is it time you returned that book?) that the breaking of it is trivial. For every time a promise is broken the complex web of human relationships which we call 'life' is given another wrench and the damage done goes far beyond the first parties involved.

The relationship which most obviously and publicly rests on promise is marriage. 'I will,' they say. Seven, eighteen or twenty-five years later that promise is put to the test. Another woman appears or the children have left home or interests are no longer shared or some ambition of the husband is not accepted by the wife and the promises are swept aside as so much clutter. If a marriage looks like breaking up you hear lots about being adult and realistic or the effect it has on the children. What you do not hear about is the fact that if the marriage dissolves then the parties are *dishonoured*. Like a man who dishonours his cheque, they will not fulfil what they promised. Recently a theologian writing in a newspaper suggested that marriage could be regarded as 'a soluble covenant.' What I can say is that if God makes 'soluble covenants' then I shall go to hell for sure. My only hope is that his word is irrevocable and will not change.

DEALING WITH 'HUMAN NATURE'

Everybody wants stable relationships with other people and 'stable' does not mean 'dull.' We need each other in order to become ourselves. The child in the family needs a strong relationship with his parents; husband and wife need to be sure of each other; friends should stick to each other in loyalty; there should be trust between master and man; governments should enjoy the confidence of those they rule; managers of football teams should be loved by their players; vicars and organists should work in harmony. And it is these very qualities which come from being justified by grace. Saying sorry, telling the truth, keeping promises – these are the characteristics which come directly from the man who receives as a gift from God all that he has and is. There is no gap between theology and practice. Like the unforgiving servant if we do not understand what God is saying we shall act wrongly. But if we believe and understand what God is doing for us, then we shall become like him. The old pagan dream that there is somewhere a drink that will make man immortal finds its substance in the grace of Christ. The drink is to accept 'we are saved by grace through faith.' It is not easy to drain the cup to the bottom for in the process I must admit that I am nothing and I can do nothing. And my old nature fights against admitting anything like it. The first sin, Adam's sin, was disobedience. 'I will do what I want because I know better.' It is the sin of the three year old: self-will, pride. And from this elemental self-centredness come all our attitudes which Paul calls 'the old nature,' 'the lower nature,' 'the flesh,' 'human nature.'

And so a man becomes an enemy of God when his mind is controlled by human nature; for he does not obey God's Law, and in fact he cannot obey it. Those who obey their human nature cannot please God.   *Romans 8:7, 8*

Suppose a prefect in the sixth form at school is accused by a boy in a lower form of omitting his name from a list. Immediately the prefect feels angry and resentful. His pride is outraged. 'What right has this whipper-snapper to tell me off?' As a matter of fact the junior is correct but that does not stop his superior from getting angry. This happens every day in government offices, in businesses, in schools and colleges, on the building site and in the factory: men being righteously indignant. It makes you feel good to get angry and feel yourself to be in the right at the same time. You hate being criticised and if your critic is below you then you can get angry at his impertinence and divert attention from your own behaviour. But the Christian need not react in this fashion for he is one who welcomes the truth whoever it comes from.

But pride in man is so strong that even when we are criticised by our superiors we still feel resentment. They have every right to reprove us, indeed they would be failing in their duty if they did not reprove us. Yet we hate criticism and we try to excuse ourselves in self-justification. But I cannot justify myself! That is the whole point of receiving God's justification as a gift. So if I cannot justify myself before God why should I try to do so before men?

Two men in a business firm are more or less level with each other. A higher post falls vacant and one of them is promoted to fill it. The reaction of the other is swift. First, envy: 'I wish I could be him!'; then resentment: 'Surely the management can see that I'm a better man!'; finally jealousy: 'I will do everything I can to discredit this fellow.' Pride in jealousy can be so violent, so consuming a passion that the person suffering from it feels almost physically sick with anger. His jealousy is inflamed by covetousness when he sees that the other man is now able to enjoy power and possessions denied to him.

The classic Bible instance of jealousy is Saul, first King of Israel. His descent to suicide begins with disobedience to God. Envy of David's success in battle leads him further down the slope. Then the burning jealousy which turns him against his own son Jonathan and the self-pity he feels as he is convinced that nobody is loyal to him only increase the slide. With his attempts to murder David and the remorse he feels, Saul is treading a dangerous path which can only lead to destruction. At the beginning of the story Saul is depicted as a fine man: modest, wise, humble, brave, able to make decisions, generous. And at the end he is proud, petulant, distrustful, jealous, mean in his judgments, vacillating and despairing. He begins by trust in God: he ends by consulting a spiritualist. On his school report would have been written 'He shows promise.' The promise was not fulfilled.

These stories are not illustrations of disaster but demonstrations. This is what will happen to us if we follow human nature instead of becoming like Jesus. If we do not give God first place we can be sure that pride will give it to us. Pride is the disease and it is fatal: it is destructive of all that you hope to be and to do. The other things (and you will find lists in Galatians 5 and Romans 13) envy, jealousy, gossiping, forming cliques, planning revenge, self-pity, judging others are symptoms of the disease. Treating the symptoms will make you socially acceptable and as discipline this is good. But the Christian's great need is to put self to death; to lose for ever the desire to be distinguished above other men; to think nothing of one's own reputation and status. The daily inscription over the Christian's life should be 'expecting nothing in return.'

For this drastic revolution to take place two things need to happen. First, the Christian must drink deeply of justification by faith only. Secondly, the Holy Spirit must come into his life to provide the power to live out that teaching in daily relationships.

LOVING YOUR ENEMIES

To conclude, let us again consider the words of our Lord written in Luke 6:35: 'Love your enemies and do good to them; lend and expect nothing back. You will have a great reward, and you will be sons of the Most High God. For he is good to the ungrateful and the wicked.'

So far we have been thinking of how to make and keep friends; inside and outside the Church; in marriage; in school; in our working life. But the gospel does not stop there. We have a *world* commitment. Having discovered slowly and painfully how to go on living with our relatives and friends, God calls us to the most amazing pattern of all: he says we are to love our enemies. Of course it's impossible. But the reason God asks it of us is that he is like that. What short memories we have! Only a little while ago we were God's enemies and yet he sent Christ to us to bring us into his family. Think of St Paul. He was bitterly opposed to the Christian message, to the Church, to all that God was doing. But God did not stop loving him and how grateful he was:

Christ Jesus came into the world to save sinners. I am the worst of them, but it was for this very reason that God was merciful to me, in order that Christ Jesus might show his full patience in dealing with me, the worst of sinners. *I Timothy 1:15, 16*

Now if God is like that to you, you should be like that to others. Jesus says, 'Be merciful, just as your Father is merciful.'

Impossible? Well, I am amazed that in fact it is possible. Richard Wurmbrand, the Rumanian Christian who spent fourteen years as a prisoner of the Communists, wrote these words:

A flower, if you bruise it under your feet, rewards you by giving you its perfume. Likewise Christians, tortured by the Communists, rewarded their torturers by love. We brought many of our jailors to Christ. And we are dominated by one desire: to give to the Communists who have made us suffer the best which we have, the salvation which comes from our Lord Jesus Christ.

Strictly speaking it is not true that we expect *nothing* in return; for by love we hope that love will be returned. And just as a loving Jesus waited patiently for the return of the disloyal Peter, so we must wait in patience always open to receive those who have wronged us.

Bible quotations for Chapter 5

NOTHING IN RETURN

If you love only the people who love you, why should you expect a blessing? . . . No! Love your enemies and do good to them; lend and expect nothing back. You will have a great reward and you will be sons of the Most High God. For he is good to the ungrateful and the wicked. *Luke 6:32, 35*

Do not pay back evil with evil, or cursing with cursing; instead pay back with a blessing, because a blessing is what God promised to give you when he called you. *I Peter 3:9*

FORGIVING OTHERS

No more shouting or insults! No more hateful feelings of any sort! Instead be kind and tender-hearted to one another, and forgive one another, as God has forgiven you in Christ. *Ephesians 4:31, 32*

TELLING THE TRUTH

Do not lie to one another, for you have put off the old self with its habits, and have put on the new self. This is the new man which God, its creator, is constantly renewing in his own image, to bring you to a full knowledge of himself. *Colossians 3:9, 10*

Whoever wants to enjoy life and wishes to see good times, must keep from speaking evil, and stop telling lies. *I Peter 3:10*

KEEPING YOUR PROMISES

Who shall dwell on thy holy hill? . . .
he who swears to his own hurt and does not change. *Psalm 15:1, 4 (RSV)*

Your friend and your father's friend, do not forsake. *Proverbs 27:10 (RSV)*

You have also heard that men were told in the past, 'Do not break your promise, but do what you have sworn to the Lord to do.' But now I tell you. . . . Just say 'Yes' or 'No' – anything else you have to say comes from the Evil One. *Matthew 5:33, 37*

DEALING WITH 'HUMAN NATURE'

To have your mind controlled by what human nature wants will result in death; to have your mind controlled by the Spirit results in life and peace. . . . Those who obey their human nature cannot please God. *Romans 8:6, 8*

LOVING YOUR ENEMIES

They kept on stoning Stephen as he called on the Lord, 'Lord Jesus, receive my spirit!' He knelt down and cried in a loud voice, 'Lord! Do not remember this sin against them!' He said this and died. *Acts 7:59, 60*

Do not take revenge on someone who does you wrong. If anyone slaps you on the right cheek, let him slap your left cheek too. *Matthew 5:39*

Questions for discussion

1   Why is it so difficult to forgive people when they wrong us? Is it possible to forget as well as to forgive?

2   People these days think little of backing out of a promise if it suits their purpose. Can it ever be right to break a promise?

3   Which is worse: murder or jealousy?

6

The world's squeeze

'I walked into the room and do you know, I was the only girl there in a short dress. I could have died!'

What a humiliating thing it is to feel conspicuous! Of course, there are a few extroverts who just revel in being different but for most of us there is a social mechanism which demands that we conform. I was once on a houseparty with some young people and we had organised a Communion service with all the chairs in one large circle so that there were just enough chairs for the number coming. I was one of the last to arrive and I can remember the feeling, on entering the room, of being 'outside the circle.' For those who had left it later than I had, their embarrassment on arrival was even greater, especially if they could not immediately see a vacant chair. And you could almost feel the sigh of relief when they found their place and were able to merge into the general setting. It is not only animals who like to camouflage themselves in their surroundings.

Well, I have bad news for Christians. To a greater or less extent you are always going to stick out like a sore thumb in the world and there will be many times when you feel painfully conspicuous. And your whole social make-up will scream and protest. 'I don't want to be different.' – 'Why can't I be normal?' – 'Do I *have* to speak of Christ when I meet people?' – 'I feel such a goody-goody' – and so on. No one wants to stick out in a crowd for other people to comment on. One of the most spectacular pieces of 'sticking out' in Christian history was when the Emperor Nero tied Christians on to poles, daubed them with pitch and set them alight to act as torches at night. It was both uncomfortable and conspicuous. But that is just how Christians are frequently made to feel, when the standards of behaviour and speech of people around them are so different from their own. The Christian's world commitment, then, is painful. No one will thank him for being committed to the world or for bringing his message. What the world will do is to exercise every trick of the trade to break down the Christian and get him to conform to its own pattern.

It should not come as a surprise. After all, look what the world did to Jesus: it hated him and killed him. And a servant is not greater than his master. Jesus warned his disciples before he left them:

If the world hates you, you must remember that it has hated me first. If you belonged to the world, then the world would love you as its own. But I chose you from this world, and you do not belong to it; this is why the world hates you. . . . And the time will come when anyone who kills you will think that by doing this he is serving God.   *John 15:18–25*

Open opposition, then, is something we should expect and, surprisingly enough, something that it is possible to cope with in God's strength once we have taken a stand. For instance, many a young person away from home has found that if he kneels down and says his prayers at night in front of others then it is not too bad once the plunge is taken. If the opposition is open and verbal it is at least possible to meet it. What is so difficult is to resist the pressure to conform which comes from the world in subtle and hidden ways. So often the Enemy overwhelms our defences in attitudes and presuppositions which we fail to criticise because we absorb them without noticing or thinking. These attitudes can be caught from parents, from school teachers, from our contemporaries, even from other Christians who have failed to notice that their thinking is the world's thinking. 'But everybody does it' is so often the cry. We can be sure that God's requirements are not based on such a saying. That's what they said on the day when everyone shouted 'Crucify him!'

MONEY AND THINGS

Young people often feel that money is the way to a full, successful life. Money can buy us things which we feel must be satisfying; and enough money brings its own power which enables us to fulfil our ambitions. In considering a career, it is almost the first question to be asked, 'How much is the salary?' And the second is, 'What are the prospects of promotion?', in other words 'What chance is there of the salary increasing?' No one in the world thinks any the worse of you for asking these questions. It is just assumed that they are the normal and proper questions to ask. The assumption is 'Money leads to happiness' and if you believe that then already the world has squeezed you into its way of thinking.

Consider our attitude to new people in our neighbourhood. More often than not we want to know their monetary value rather than their spiritual value. A company director with two cars and a big house is more likely to have the doors of the club (or the church!) thrown open to him than a labourer from the council estate. Then what about the boy who comes along in a new sports car of his own? He is guaranteed almost instant success. He certainly will not lack friends of either sex. Or there is the family with a colour television. Wealth is like a magnet and all of us are drawn to it. We may affect to despise these people and their wealthy status symbols, but we cannot help respecting them. After all, we think, have they not found the key to success?

It will take a great deal of determination on your part to *believe* what Jesus said about riches. By 'believe' I mean 'base your life upon.' For what Jesus says is clean contrary to what the world thinks. Here are some of his arguments:

● All possessions and riches are *temporary*. Moth gets at clothes, rust at metal and thieves get at everything else. So if you put your confidence in something that is temporary sooner or later you will be let down.

● He attacks the very idea of 'possession.' After all even if you own something 'permanent,' like a piece of land, will it still belong to you when you die? I once saw an inscription on a wall in Suffolk: 'This wall belongs to W. N. Nolloth built 1884.' The absurdity of this statement is seen when you realise that sooner or later the statement becomes false, that the idea of a permanent possession is a self-contradiction.

● This leads to the conclusion that a man cannot be measured by his possessions. If you judge what a man is by what he has, you are bound to be making a mistake. What is worse you have become 'partial,' quite unlike God who ignores a man's riches in arriving at his worth.

● A man starts by owning his money but in the end his money

owns him. His desire for money is insatiable: he wants more and more. So money becomes his Master. Listen to Joe Lampton from *Room at the Top*, John Braine's novel about an ambitious, ruthless young man:

I wanted an Aston-Martin, I wanted an expensive linen shirt, I wanted a girl with a Riviera suntan, these were my rights I felt. ... I made my choice then and there: I was going to enjoy all the luxuries which that young man enjoyed.

● To have too much money is to threaten your Christian life. For riches are distracting, they will choke the Word of God like the thistles choke the corn. And riches are worrying and will make you full of care and anxiety. So Jesus proclaims,

> How terrible for you who are rich now
> you have had your easy life! *Luke 6:24*

> Happy are you poor:
> the Kingdom of God is yours! *Luke 6:20*

Our whole society teaches the opposite. Advertising continually stimulates our desire for things and so our longing for more money. Letters come through the post offering £1500; television programmes show people carrying off the loot; football pools offer us short cuts to happiness; the news is all of pay-rises and settlements. And behind it all a vast substructure of investment, profitability and greed. Oh, that's only human, you say. Yes, and we are all infected with it. When we become Christians we are rescued from the present Age which would drag us away from God. And yet we flirt with the love of money, still imagining that somehow our life's happiness is bound up with it. It is not! Even the Beatles sang 'Money can't buy me love.'

This modern idolatry is the alternative religion to Christianity in the West. A Christian young man would not dream of worshipping Buddha, yet he thinks nothing of spending all his spare time working to buy a hi-fi outfit. He would not dream of practising as a Hindu, yet he lives for his collection of records. The young Christian girl would never be found spreading the teaching of Jehovah's Witnesses, yet she spends most of her time talking about clothes – and the amount she spends on cosmetics would feed a baby in India. Possessions have a frightful habit of moving in and taking us over. You can be so obsessed with your camera that you can't look at views or people, only the pictures they would make.

Men lie under their cars all day maintaining them. Women spend hours of shopping time looking for knick-knacks and then many more hours dusting them. Decide now! What are you going to fill your life with? 'Love God and love your neighbour' is the Christian way: keep money and things firmly in their place as instruments of love.

'SCIENCE SOLVES EVERYTHING'

No one denies that the growth of the sciences has eased our lives enormously. If you can remember washing up dishes before detergents were invented then you will remember what a messy business it used to be.

The ability to build giant molecules to order enabling us to construct new materials with required characteristics has brought about a revolution in our daily living with plastics. Improved technology gives us more energy, more gadgets, more reliable transport and the instant communication of the telephone and television. There is no question at all that life in the Britain of the 1970s has some fascinating and useful advantages over life in Britain in the 1870s. When the missionaries went to Uganda in the last century it took them three months or more to walk from the coast as well as the time for the sea passage to Zanzibar. Today, the same journey can be done in about nine hours from London.

Christians, like the rest, take advantage of the increased comfort which comes from increased knowledge. But it would be a mistake to think that all problems can be solved 'scientifically.' Perhaps the most spectacular achievement of science has been the sending of men to the moon. Yet one of those men, Colonel Aldrin, records that a year after splashdown in the Pacific in July 1969, he began suffering from recurrent bouts of 'devastating depression alternating with brief emotional heights.' Science to the rescue: Colonel Aldrin was admitted to a mental hospital. But what was uncovered was purposelessness, loneliness and disenchantment caused by travelling. Psychiatry may indeed analyse a man but his deepest needs will be met outside science.

I do not deny that psychology, properly applied, can solve some problems. But so many of the problems we face are *spiritual* problems, things like lack of purpose, guilt, pride, anxiety, covetousness, hatred. And these are the problems of daily living. They are not *scientific* problems at all and part of the proof of this is that 'scientists' have them as well as the rest of us. They are problems which arise from not being related to God and not being open to his wisdom. And they are problems which lead to further difficulties when we try to relate creatively to our fellow men.

Ethical problems like rudeness, stealing and foul language will never be solved scientifically. At first sight it sounds as though the relatively new study of sociology will answer our society's difficulties. But sociology is primarily a descriptive study and tells you what does in fact happen: it is right outside its terms of reference to say what ought to happen. Society's goals will be decided by ethical values and these, for the Christian, will be decided by the teaching of Jesus.

'GET OUT OF MY WAY'

One of the most exhilarating experiences for a young person is to learn how to drive. If you have been nothing but a cyclist or a walker all your life, it is with a real sense of liberation that you take the wheel. But driving, especially in a town, can be quite a shocking experience. First there is the aggressive behaviour of other drivers. Given half a chance they will edge you off the road. You have to learn to get well out into the road to turn right otherwise you will find yourself trapped on the nearside kerb trying in vain to cross the traffic. On a narrow road in the rush-hour the impatient ones will form a second lane of traffic on your right and then, when the road inevitably narrows, force their way in front of you. Indeed if you leave a sensible gap between yourself and the car in front in no time two or three will have nipped in.

But even worse there is the discovery of what sort of person you are! If you are walking along a pavement and someone suddenly gets in the way you find you have learnt to control your language if not your thoughts. But in a similar situation in a car it is as though your cranium has expanded to the walls of the car and you now speak out loud what were previously only thoughts in your head. 'Get out of my way'; 'You idiot! Can't you drive better than that?' 'Crazy woman! What did she do that for?'; 'Will you get a move on! I can't hang about all day!'; 'The swine! Look how he cut in on me then!' The point is very clear: on the 'inside' your attitudes have hardly changed at all. As a Christian you have probably tidied up your outside, but inside the aggression you criticise in others is still part of your human nature. Shameful, indeed, and when you get married you will be appalled to hear the things the children say in copying you. Jesus said:

You have heard that men were told in the past 'Do not murder' . . . But now I tell you: whoever is angry with his brother will be brought before the judge; and whoever calls his brother a worthless fool will be in danger of going to the fire of hell. *Matthew 5:21, 22*

If those words were the law of the United Kingdom, every motorist would be in court, for who could say he had not broken them? But we shall be in court one day, and the judge will be God.

'HE'S ONLY AN AFRICAN'

Earlier on I said that we loved to think of everyone as 'below' us and that we bolster our own pride by pointing out the defects of others. One aspect of this is racialism. I did not really understand how racialist I was until I went to live in Africa. I found myself doing this kind of thing: I would queue up at the Post Office to buy stamps and find that the queue moved very slowly. I would then get irritated and mutter something like, 'Oh, these Africans. They're so slow!' And then I noticed that if I had to wait in a Post Office in England for an equally long time (and it does sometimes happen) I would mutter, 'That woman is very slow.' You see the point? What I did *not* say was, 'Oh these English. They are so lazy!' I would not willingly make a condemnation of my own country-man, because I am one! I suppose I *might* say, 'Oh these civil servants . . .' but only if I was not one myself. These sweeping statements of scorn, therefore, are convenient ways of building my own pride. And it's so easy if the other group is a different colour from me!

Now in some ways many Africans are less educated and less technologically developed than Europeans. But there are good and bad, clever and stupid, amusing and dull Africans, just as there are different types of Englishmen. What is required of me is a sober estimate of each man and an avoidance of completely dismissing as worthless a whole section of the race. I have met Africans who, in intellectual power, are streets ahead of me; and I know Africans who work harder than I do; and I know Africans who are better Christians than I am. Where then is my racialist pride? As a matter of history Europeans have not a great deal to be proud of in Africa. No, they were not *all* 'colonial exploiters.' To say that would be racialist again and it is intriguing to see how some intellectuals have fallen into this inverted pride. But the imagined or pretended superiority of many of our fellow-countrymen is most unrealistic.

There is an example of racialist prejudice in John chapter 4. Jews and Samaritans have no dealings with each other, so the woman (a Samaritan) is astonished when Jesus (a Jew) talks with her and asks for a drink. When Jesus's disciples return they are 'greatly surprised to find him talking with a woman. But none of them said to her "What do you want" or asked him "Why are you talking with her?" ' (John 4:27). The world's prejudice is here, right in the disciples. They have inherited their ancestors' views of the Samaritans. Not so Jesus. He has not been squeezed by the world but carves out his own course, as love dictates.

THEY WON'T MISS IT
No one would think of putting his hand into his friend's jacket pocket and stealing fifty pence. But few would scruple to leave work five minutes early every day for a week. It has been suggested that pilfering and fraud partly spring from people's readiness to regard the state and the mammoth commercial companies as 'things' or unfeeling organisations. There is no sense of personal injury when you steal from a large impersonal company, they say. No doubt there is some truth in this but the world's motto is, 'It's not wrong if you don't get caught.' And let's face it: if there was something which you very much wanted to do and you were told that there was absolutely no chance that you would be found out, it would take a great deal of determination to resist. And if you are dealing with a large organisation there may be less chance of your being detected.

Some years ago I was in a restaurant and when the waiter came to write out the bill he deliberately omitted some of the items and said, 'That's all right.' I didn't protest: the bill already was colossal so I paid at the cash desk and went out. I got outside and suddenly it hit me: what had I done? The waiter was not the proprietor, it was not *his* money he was giving away! I had deliberately under-paid for the meal. Immediately, self-justification erupted. 'It was too expensive, anyway. They must be making an enormous profit in this place. It wasn't *my* fault he wrote out the bill wrong. I didn't ask him' and so forth. Well, it was a tough struggle but eventually I did go back and pay for the omitted items. There have been other times, I think, when I was not so honest. The world shouts at us, 'If you're not caught it's all right. Everybody does it.'

There is a fascinating little story in Genesis 39. Joseph, far from home, out of his context, is the privileged servant in a rich Egyptian household. One day his master's wife asks him to go to bed with her. He refuses but she persists with her immoral proposal day after day. Joseph's reply is, 'How then can I do this great wickedness and sin against God?'

Sooner or later we give in to the world's pressure unless we remember that we belong to a God who is over all and who sees all. To put the situation at its crudest: you *will* get caught. There *is* no getting away with it for finally you are accountable to God, not to human judges. And God has appointed a day when you will meet him.

PROVE IN PRACTICE

In this chapter I have indicated some of the ways in which the world wishes to force its thinking into the Christian. Here are a few more, which you might like to think about and work out the Christian answer:

● I'm only a cog in the machine.
● All religions are the same.
● God helps those who help themselves.
● It doesn't matter: there is nothing you can do.
● Mind your own business.
● You must look after No. 1.
● I never had a chance.
● A little of what you fancy does you good.
● You're not a man till you've had a woman.
● Let him stew in his own juice.
● You're nearer to God in a garden than anywhere else on earth.
● Jesus was a good man.

Well, it is hard work resisting the world, but it is part of your devotion to Christ. Here are Paul's words:

Don't let the world around you squeeze you into its own mould, but let God remould your minds from within, so that you may prove in practice that the plan of God for you is good.   *Romans 12:2 (JBP)*

Bible quotations for Chapter 6

THE WORLD'S SQUEEZE

Don't let the world around you squeeze you into its own mould.

Romans 12:2(JBP)

Happy are you if you are insulted because you are Christ's followers; this means that the glorious spirit, the spirit of God, is resting on you. None of you should suffer because he is a murderer, or a thief, or a criminal, or tries to manage other people's business. But if you suffer because you are a Christian, don't be ashamed of it, but thank God that you bear Christ's name. *1 Peter 4:14–16*

MONEY AND THINGS

But God said to him, 'You fool! This very night you will have to give up your life; then who will get all these things you have kept for yourself?' *Luke 12:20*

And Jesus concluded, 'This is how it is with those who pile up riches for themselves but are not rich in God's sight.' *Luke 12:21*

Do not save riches here on earth, where moths and rust destroy, and robbers break in and steal. Instead save riches in heaven. *Matthew 6:19, 20*

You cannot serve both God and Money. *Matthew 6:24*

'SCIENCE SOLVES EVERYTHING'

For God in his wisdom made it impossible for men to know him by means of their own wisdom. Instead, God decided to save those who believe, by means of the 'foolish' message we preach. *I Corinthians 1:21*

'GET OUT OF MY WAY'

Deliver me, O Lord, from evil men;
preserve me from violent men
Who plan evil things in their heart,
and stir up wars continually. *Psalm 140:1, 2 (RSV)*

'HE'S ONLY AN AFRICAN'

Blessed is the man who walks not in the counsel of the wicked
nor stands in the way of sinners
nor sits in the seat of scoffers. *Psalm 1:1 (RSV)*

Towards the scorners, (the Lord) is scornful. *Proverbs 3:34 (RSV)*

Peter began to speak 'I now realise that it is true that God treats all men alike. . . .' *Acts 10:34*

'THEY WON'T MISS IT'

They crush thy people, O Lord . . .
They slay the widow . . .
and they say 'The Lord does not see; the God of Jacob does not perceive.' *Psalm 94:5–7 (RSV)*

Whatever is covered up will be uncovered, and every secret will be made known. So then, whatever you have said in the dark will be heard in broad daylight, and whatever you have whispered in men's ears in a closed room will be shouted from the housetops.   *Luke 12:2, 3*

DO NOT LOVE THE WORLD

Everything that belongs to the world – what the sinful self desires, what people see and want, and everything in this world that people are so proud of – none of this comes from the Father; it all comes from the world.

The world and everything in it that men desire is passing away; but he who does what God wants lives for ever.   *I John 2:16, 17*

Put all things to the test: keep what is good, and avoid every kind of evil.
                                                                        I Thessalonians 5:21, 22

Questions for discussion

1   What is the difference between being conspicuous because you are a Christian and being conspicuous because you are an awkward character?

2   Is it possible to enjoy the good things of life and still be a Christian?

3   Discuss one of the slogans in the section 'Prove in practice.'

7
Led by the Spirit

Sometimes life seems to be like a locked box with the key inside: you have to get inside before you can open it. It is when you are young that you have to make some of your greatest decisions: who you will marry, what training you will have, which job you will accept. So you need all the wisdom you can get in order to decide rightly but wisdom is not a commodity found in enormous quantities in young people.

Think for a moment of the difficulty of choosing a wife. You need someone who will fit the irregular shape of your own character. I do not mean someone exactly like you but someone who will be *good* for you. We take it for granted that she will love you and be kind to you but the aim is to create a couple who will develop and strengthen each other. Now at the age of twenty-two or so, neither of you has a developed personality and so, in the strictest sense, nobody knows as yet who you are or what your potential is. Some of your biggest problems will arise when you are forty or fifty years old but how can you tell *now* what those problems will be? So we have two unknown personalities x and y and a problematic z which is how they will react on each other and we propose to make a life commitment between them. Put like that, it's a wonder anyone dares to get married at all, and it's not surprising if many people consider a trial marriage before finally committing themselves.

Of course, in practice, no one is so intellectual about the choice and our emotions come to the rescue and sweep us into marriage or at the very least tide us over the difficult moments. But it *is* a big decision and an important one and we are foolish if we take it on 'lightly or unadvisedly' as the Prayer Book says. Similarly, deciding on a course of training or accepting a certain post has enormous implications for your future and a wrong decision now can mean decades of misery or less-than-the-best in the future. So what are you to do in the Big Decisions? You cannot do better than take at its face value the promise of God:

But if any of you lacks wisdom, he should pray to God, who will give it to him; for God gives generously and graciously to all. *James 1:5*

God knows all things which means that he knows the end from the beginning. He knows exactly what your personality and your potential are. He knows the sort of thing you will be coming up against in future; he knows the type of girl who will, humanly speaking, meet your needs; perhaps, most important of all, he knows what good he wants to do in and through you, a good that he cannot do through anyone else because you are unique. Up to now I have talked as though the point is a negative one, that all we are concerned about is avoiding problems and difficulties. God's plan is more positive than that! His plan is that you should be fruitful, that is, useful to him and to others. He has a *destiny* for you which he is longing to fulfil in you for the benefit of others and yourself.

You will not find this destiny by yourself. You cannot know what it is (nor could you fulfil it if you *did* know it), unless God is showing you and guiding you. And it is your being joined to God that will make you who you ought to be. Jesus says, 'Remain in union with me, and I will remain in union with you. Unless you remain in me you cannot bear fruit, just as a branch cannot bear fruit unless it remains in the vine.' So your way ahead is to pray for wisdom; pray that God will guide you and show you the way; and so to be joined to Christ that you will share the plans which he has already made for you.

The passage in James goes on to emphasise the importance of praying in faith. What is it that you must believe if you are to receive God's wisdom?

YOU MUST BELIEVE THAT GOD LOVES YOU AND WANTS YOU TO HAVE HIS BEST

It is strange how we retain pagan views of God, and in particular the view that 'the gods don't like to see men too happy.' Unconsciously, perhaps, we assume that the duty which God is going to place on us will be wearisome and dreary. The most difficult time to believe that God wants the best for you is when his commandments forbid a certain course of action that you desperately want to follow. Can you believe that the commandments are there to *protect* you from second-best? For instance a young man or woman may be tempted to have sex before getting married. The Bible says, 'No fornication.' Can the Christian believe that to obey God is to get the best? 'Oh, but you see, we *are* going to get married.' That's irrelevant: obey the Word! 'But I don't want to!' Then are you sure that you *believe* the Word? Do you believe that God framed those commandments to give you the best?

It's the same when you think of God's plan for your whole life. Suddenly your parents move, or you fail a vital examination. It seems as though life has fallen apart. Your girlfriend throws you over and life stretches before you, grey and uninviting. God loves you! Believe it. It is wonderful how he works things out. I feel this especially about failed examinations. We tend to see them as a wall beyond which is a delectable garden. Once over the wall we shall be happy. But this is not necessarily true. If, by a tremendous effort, you pass an examination that is too difficult for you, you may find yourself in a job or career that is beyond your capabilities: and that is to be in a really miserable situation. Sometimes then the examination is a wall but beyond is a desert. The wall is God's mercy to keep you out of an unpleasant life.

YOU MUST BELIEVE THAT GOD WANTS TO COMMUNICATE WITH YOU AND IS ABLE TO COMMUNICATE WITH YOU

The God of the Bible is the One who speaks. If you read the story of Moses or Jeremiah or Joshua you will find it recorded that God *spoke* and guided his people. And having spoken to us through the prophets he sent to us his Son, Jesus. John called him 'the Word,' that is to say, 'God wants to communicate with you.'

Now there are times when you are looking for guidance but there seems to be nothing but silence. There is no indication at all of what God wants: it is as though the doors are shut and you are hammering on them with your bare fists. You get desperate. Why doesn't he speak? Perhaps he can't speak! Perhaps he's not interested in me. Come on, be realistic! How can I, in my insignificance, have a claim on the attention of the Almighty of the Universe? In their desperation Christians sometimes look for a supernormal happening. They hope to hear a voice or see something written in the sky. They may go to a prophet hoping to receive just the right form of words which reveals God's will. Sometimes they put off making a decision because 'no guidance has come' while the situation is crying out for a decision to be made. It is at moments like these when we must go on believing that he *does* care, he *can* speak and he *will* speak! We must believe that he has not changed, that he is still the God who sends his Spirit who will guide us into all truth.

YOU MUST BE WILLING TO DO WHAT HE WANTS

At first sight this seems to be nothing to do with faith; but being willing is actually part of faith. If you stop in a strange town and ask the way to the Post Office, listen carefully to the instructions, write them down and then walk in the opposite direction, you show quite clearly that you do not believe the man trying to help you. If you ask for guidance you must be willing to put it into effect. There is a devastating story at the end of Jeremiah in chapters 42 and 43. Jeremiah was in Jerusalem after the city had been taken by the Chaldeans and a few of those who were left came to him and asked him for a word from God about whether or not they should go into Egypt. They said to Jeremiah 'Pray to the Lord for us . . . that the Lord your God may show us the way we should go . . . whether it is good or evil, we will obey the voice of the Lord our God!' It sounds as though these people were willing and absolutely ready to do whatever God should command. Ten days later God's word came to Jeremiah that the people were to stay put and not to go to Egypt and Jeremiah duly delivered the message. The reaction was violent: 'You are telling a lie. The Lord our God did *not* send you to say "Do not go to Egypt to stay there." ' What an about-face! You feel like shaking them in their wilfulness. But it is not difficult to understand their attitude. What they had said to themselves in effect was this: 'It seems great sense to go to Egypt and because it looks right to us it must be God's will. Anyway we will ask and then we'll be quite sure.' Jeremiah's reply was a bombshell but it made no difference. They had already decided what God wanted, indeed they had convinced themselves that they *knew* what God wanted, therefore Jeremiah was a liar. These men while professing to be doing God's will, turned out to be flatly disobeying God.

What a warning there is for us here. There is a brand of Christianity about these days with a great emphasis on *personal* experience. Splendid! Would that all God's people were anxious to know him first-hand. But it *can* go like this: 'I know God for myself, I know his will, I know exactly what he has said to me; therefore if anyone disagrees with me he does not know God, he is from the devil.' In such cases, the words 'So the Lord led me . . .' have now become an arrogant, blanket approval for anything I want to do. None of us is infallible and to pretend to be so can, at times, be very near blasphemy. Be careful how you take the Lord's name on your lips especially when disagreeing with a fellow-Christian. It would be disastrous to find that you had been trying to dictate to God instead of being submissive to his will.

What do you think he might ask of you? It might be something that seems impossibly hard: like remaining unmarried, or going to work in the Sahara desert, or spending ten years in study while you qualify. But he will help you with the hardness of it. It might be something that looks very hum-drum, like settling down in a London suburb, or staying in the village where you were born. Watch out, your greatest enemy is yourself. For by deliberately chasing your own wishes, you may do yourself out of the satisfying life that God has planned for you. So why not submit? The wife who has a loving husband has little difficulty in submitting to him, for all that he plans is for her benefit. It is thus against her self-interest to be self-willed.

So far, then, I have described the Christian's assumptions about being guided: he must know himself to lack the necessary wisdom; he must believe that God wants to guide him and make him wise; he must be willing to go wherever he is sent and do whatever he is asked. But how does the voice of God actually come to us? Do we see a finger in the sky or hear a voice from heaven? Here are four of the ways in which God may speak to you:

THE VOICE OF SCRIPTURE

If you say that you want to come close to the mind of God, to stand in his council and hear his voice, then your best introduction is through the people who have known him well. There are few more important things for a new Christian to do than to apply himself to Bible reading and study. He might do it on his own or in groups, with a commentary or just the text alone, but all the while he will be absorbing the attitudes and wisdom of godly men. This is such obvious good sense, though it is surprising how little value some Christians place on it.

There is a verse in Proverbs which goes like this:

'In all your ways acknowledge him and he will make straight your paths.'

3:6 (RSV)

This means that the big decisions depend on the little decisions; that you become a man of God by daily attention to the detail of his commands. Then you will be able to perceive his larger plan. If someone becomes a Christian at eighteen and then at twenty-five comes in a great panic saying, 'What shall I do? What shall I do?' then in a sense it is too late. Because if in those seven years he has been deliberately and painstakingly reading his Bible and putting it into practice, then God will 'straighten his paths.' But if he has not been 'acknowledging God in all his ways' then turning to an older Christian friend at the last minute could be merely a way of avoiding responsibility.

In Proverbs 8:13 it says 'the fear of the Lord is hatred of evil' and in 9:10 'the fear of the Lord is the beginning of wisdom.' Taken together the meaning is plain: if you will not listen to God's word in the basic morality of life, how will you listen when he tells you to go and live in Outer Mongolia? It is hypocritical to say, 'If only God would show me whether to do Arts or Sciences, I would choose the right one' if the whole set of your life is to ignore what God *has* revealed about, say, giving a proportion of your money to support church work. The acquiring of wisdom, then, is not just a moment of blinding insight, a sudden vision of God but a daily discipline. Wisdom says:

> Happy is the man who listens to me
> watching daily at my gates
> waiting beside my doors.   *Proverbs 8:34*

THE VOICE OF THE CHURCH

One of the great joys of the group-commitment is that when you need them, there are many friends to whom you can turn and with whom you can discuss your decisions. It will be a foolish Christian, indeed, who shuts himself away and says, 'This is a matter only between me and the Lord.' God has placed us in a body and your decision will affect that body. This becomes especially clear if your decision is about a career. It is of tremendous interest to the Church as to how your life is to be used and developed. You may think it is just a question of your deciding between being a chemist or a physicist: the local Christian leaders may pick you out as an obvious candidate for the ordained ministry. We live in an age of excessive individualism. Teachers are frightened of being accused of bringing 'pressure' to bear on their pupils; parents more and more are saying, 'Well, it's up to them.' A full Christian under-standing will curb this individualism. Perhaps you find that dis-tasteful, yet it is written into the Christian gospel. If Peter and Paul had to listen to the voice of the Church, who are you to say, 'It's nothing to do with them what I decide to do'?

There is one subtlety over this asking friends for advice which you have probably noticed. It is that when we have more or less made up our own minds we approach those friends who we are pretty sure will agree with our decision. We then take their advice as confirmation from God that we are doing the right thing. What we have in fact done is to dress up our own desire in religious language. There is a comic story in I Kings 22 of this kind of behaviour. In fact we might call this subtlety the 'Ahab-syndrome.' Ahab, king of Israel, is determined to go and fight at Ramoth-Gilead, but his godly partner, Jehoshaphat, from the next-door kingdom, insists that they first obtain confirmation from God through the prophets. So Ahab wheels in his prophets and (sur-prise! surprise!) they say, 'Go up and triumph; the Lord will give Ramoth-Gilead into the hand of the king.' Who are these prophets? They are time-servers and fee-earners only. They have no concern for the truth of God at all as the rest of the story shows. The result is that the king suffers a humiliating defeat and dies in the battle. You shall not take God's name in vain.

THE VOICE OF THE UNUSUAL

I am treading on delicate ground here for many Christians are convinced that it is right *and normal* for a man to look for some unusual circumstances to act as a kind of pointer to God's will. One of the difficulties of this method is that it can quickly get out of hand and produce the kind of ingenuity which is exercised by a tea-leaf reader. Supposing a man is trying to buy a house in a certain district and the name of that house is an unusual word which also happens to be the very private pet-name that the house-hunter uses for his wife. Fantastic! this is it! God is speaking to us! And if you think that far-fetched allow me to assure you that I know it to be a true instance. Or again, a man might receive an offer of a job in a certain town and an almost total stranger happens to mention that town in conversation. Here is the hand of God! But is it?

A variation of this kind of guidance is deliberately to put God to the test. A man wondering whether to replace his car says in prayer, 'Lord, if I get a letter within a week from a friend suggesting I change my car then I'll do it as from you.' I wonder really if he wouldn't get a similar result by spinning a coin. Of course, there are stories of such behaviour in the Old Testament, like Gideon putting out his fleece in Judges 6. But this does not necessarily mean that this is a Christian method. It is much more like *divination*, which was universally exercised in ancient culture but forbidden in Deuteronomy 18:10 and scorned by the prophets. It is, in reality, the religious version of the pin on the perms in football pools.

Now I must confess that when I was younger I did 'use' this method and I believe (because I did believe in God) that God did guide me. But I am increasingly unhappy about 'looking for signs.' You can make almost anything into a 'sign' if you try hard enough and all such interpretations must be strictly governed by the moral and spiritual truth of Scripture anyhow. It may be that God has pity on us in our weakness and does give us some confidence by an unusual event, but I cannot believe this is 'normal.' The Pharisees received a short sharp reply from Jesus when they asked for 'a sign.'

Before I leave this section please note that 'using the Bible' in a mechanical way is just as much divination as examining the livers of freshly-slaughtered sacrificial animals. Letting the Bible fall open and stabbing your finger on the page; pulling a promise out of a 'promise-box'; rushing to look at the text on the daily calendar: all these 'methods' sound more like consulting your horoscope than walking humbly with your God.

THE VOICE OF REASON

But the day for decision has come! You have for years soaked yourself in the Bible, you have consulted your Christian friends, you have read books and assembled as far as you can all the relevant facts. Now you must decide! How will you decide? You will decide as a reasonable Christian person.

After all it may be that your Christian friends are equally divided. It may be that there is no direct scriptural principle to guide you. It may be that no single factor in the situation stands out pointing the way forward. But you must decide for that letter must be answered today. Are we to say that God doesn't care in this particular case? Certainly not! What has happened is that you are now a mature enough Christian to be able to decide. God has given you free-will: now you must use it. It is an ability which is part of his image in you: then exercise it. You will not do so in arrogance nor in independence. You believe that God has given you his Holy Spirit who is described as a guide and you now assume you have that guidance.

Let God transform you inwardly by a complete change of your mind. Then you will be able to know the will of God – what is good, and is pleasing to him, and is perfect. *Romans 12:2*

So we decide and we rejoice. We may attach to our decision a kind of prayer like this 'Lord, I don't think I am choosing for selfish reasons. I am honestly willing to do what you want. I'm going to decide like this and you could easily stop it if you so wish. So do prevent it, if it seems good to you.' But if we did pray like this it is because we are still weak and fearful however mature we think ourselves to be. Years later we can see that the decision was a 'good' one: that is, it furthered God's purposes. And our faith in God guiding us through our reason is strengthened.

LED BY THE SPIRIT

It is the Spirit of God who sorts out our big decisions. 'Those who are led by God's Spirit are God's sons' (Romans 8:14). Obeying the leading of the Spirit will not always be enjoyable. It was the Spirit who led Jesus into the wilderness to face a time of testing. It was the Spirit who prevented Paul and Silas from going into the provinces of Asia and Bithynia and that must have been very frustrating for them. But obeying the leading of the Spirit will always be purposeful. It was the Spirit who raised up Jesus from the dead and it was the Spirit who brought Paul to Rome to preach the gospel at the centre of the Empire.

So, it's a great life! There is a plan for you and while some aspects of it are hidden, there is enough for you to make a start. You have a destiny and a God who cares about it. And with many others you will find that his will is 'perfect.'

Bible quotations for Chapter 7

LED BY THE SPIRIT
All who follow the leading of God's Spirit are God's own sons.

Romans 8:14 (JBP)

Don't be afraid! I am the first and the last. I am the living one! . . . Write then, the things you see, both the things that are now, and the things that will happen afterwards. *Revelation 1:17–19*

This is how my Father's glory is shown: by your bearing much fruit; and in this way you become my disciples. *John 15:8*

YOU MUST BELIEVE GOD LOVES YOU
We know that in all things God works for good with those who love him, those whom he has called according to his purpose. *Romans 8:28*

And I will betroth you to me for ever; I will betroth you to me in righteousness and in justice, in steadfast love and in mercy. *Hosea 2:19 (RSV)*

GOD WANTS TO COMMUNICATE
Surely the Lord God does nothing, without revealing his secret to his servants the prophets. *Amos 3:7 (RSV)*

The Word (of God) became a human being and lived among us. We saw his glory, full of grace and truth. *John 1:14*

YOU MUST BE WILLING
(Jesus said,) Whoever is willing to do what God wants will know whether what I teach comes from God or whether I speak on my own authority. *John 7:17*

Jesus answered, 'How happy are those who hear the word of God and obey it!' *Luke 11:28*

THE VOICE OF SCRIPTURE
(Jesus found guidance for his life in the Scripture) And a voice came from heaven: 'You are my own dear son. I am well pleased with you.'

Luke 3:22 quoting Psalm 2:7
and Isaiah 42:1

Then he opened their minds to understand the Scriptures, and said to them, 'This is what is written: that the Messiah must suffer and be raised from death on the third day.' *Luke 24:45, 46*

THE VOICE OF THE CHURCH
While they were serving the Lord and fasting, the Holy Spirit said to them, 'Set apart for me Barnabas and Saul, to do the work to which I have called them.' They fasted and prayed, placed their hands on them and sent them off.

Acts 13:2, 3

For all things are done according to God's plan and decision; and God chose us to be his own people in union with Christ because of his own purpose.

Ephesians 1:11

Under his control all the different parts of the body fit together. . . .

Ephesians 4:16

THE VOICE OF THE UNUSUAL

Paul had a vision that night in which he saw a man of Macedonia standing and begging him, 'Come over to Macedonia and help us!' As soon as Paul had this vision, we got ready to leave for Macedonia, because we decided that God had called us to preach the Good News to the people there. *Acts 16:9, 10*

Then some of the scribes and Pharisees said, 'Master, we want to see a sign from you.' But Jesus told them, 'It is an evil and unfaithful generation that craves for a sign and no sign will be given to it – except the sign of the prophet Jonah' (*ie* the Resurrection). *Matthew 12:38, 39 (JBP)*

THE VOICE OF REASON

For God has not given us a spirit of fear, but a spirit of power and love and a sound mind. *II Timothy 1:7 (JBP)*

The whole city in an uproar . . . *Acts 17:5*

As soon as night came, the brothers sent Paul and Silas to Berea. *Acts 17:10*

But the son of Paul's sister heard of the plot; so he went and entered the fort and told it to Paul. Then Paul called one of the officers and said to him, 'Take this young man to the commander; he has something to tell him.' *Acts 23:16, 17*

Questions for discussion

1 Just how does God communicate with men? Share your experience with others.

2 How far should your circumstances influence your decision in choosing a career?

3 How would you advise a Christian who said, 'I am willing to take a job anywhere except Manchester'?

8
His Spirit is with us

Man is a very puzzling creature. On the one hand he is an animal, with a physical body living in a very earthy and obvious world. On the other hand because he is self-conscious, is able to reflect on his experience, plan for the future and use articulate speech, he is able to reach out to God. He does so in speech, in set forms, in music, in dance. But he is not only a creature of the Word he is also a bodily creature and desires a bodily focus for his worship.

MAKING AN IMAGE

Religions all over the world show that man feels a need to particularise God. He wants to be able to point to a particular place and say, 'Here is God.' Sometimes a natural object provides the necessary focus. The Kikuyu think of the peaks of Bation and Nelion on Mount Kenya as a special place for the divinities. The Akamba have sacred trees. Widespread in ancient as well as modern culture is image-making. The word 'idol' in its origin means 'image,' and in the manufacture of idols, man is trying to contrive a situation where he is face to face with his God.

Alone among the ancient peoples, the Israelites were forbidden to make representations of God. The first of the Ten Commandments states clearly who it is who should be worshipped – the true God, the Lord himself. The second, which says, 'You shall not make a graven image' tells how he is not to be worshipped. The reason why they were told not to make an image is given in Deuteronomy 4:15, 16:

Since you saw no form on the day that the Lord spoke to you at Horeb out of the midst of the fire, beware lest you act corruptly by making a graven image for yourselves. *RSV*

90

They did not see God, so they could not make an image of him. If they made an image they would get it wrong. It would be an untruthful representation of God. And God must be worshipped in truth. But the Israelites, although they did not make images to look at, did have something to provide a bodily focus for their worship. There was the tent-shrine, later superseded by the Temple: and inside was the sacred furniture, the sideboard with bread on it, the incense altar, and the candlestick. Although the presence of God himself was not symbolised, the Holiest Place, a room cubic in form, was held to contain the presence of God. The only piece of furniture in this room was an empty throne.

In the later Jewish synagogue worship, the most important cultic object is the roll of the Law. It is kept in a tabernacle and carried around with ceremony. It is read with great reverence, the reader being checked by two other men to make sure that the Law is always read out correctly. Any copies that are made of the Law are done with scrupulous care. Although it would be most offensive to a Jew to suggest that he has made an idol of the Law, it is interesting to see the way in which it has become a focus of attention and has met the need to define and represent the characteristics of God.

THE CHRISTIAN IMAGE

We can now appreciate two things. First, there is a real need to particularise God, that is to identify him and his activity with a special bodily focus. Secondly, there is the great danger of idolatry which is both to misrepresent God and to fall into superstition. In Christianity the need is met and the danger is avoided. For *Jesus himself* is the image of God. This is no idolatry because his birth and life is the work of God's Holy Spirit: God is revealing himself. We thus have in history, on this earth a particularised God. To know Jesus is to know God. There was real personal contact between God and Man which was nothing like the unsatisfactory and mis-leading contact that a man has with an idol. For idols do not hear or speak. But Jesus was a real, warm, living person whom men could meet and touch.

But what next? Jesus died, rose again and returned to his Father. There is no longer apparently a focus for the presence of God and perhaps with the gift of the Holy Spirit there is no longer any need for one. I think there is an important point here. Christian men and women by the power of the Holy Spirit are changed into the likeness of Christ and they become images of him. If you asked me for a bodily proof of the activity of God in this world I would show you some saintly person who had lived his life for years under the influence of the Holy Spirit. I would point out the likeness of the Christian man to Jesus Christ and say, 'There you are. That is God at work.'

THE CHRISTIAN SACRAMENTS

However this still does not quite meet our need to find some tangible focus of God at work. And that is why Christ gave us the sacraments of Baptism and Communion. You can feel the water on your head; you can chew the bread and feel the wine warm in your throat; and Christ has given us these physical signs to concentrate our commitment and devotion. You can look at the bread and the wine on the Table and say to yourself:

'Why are they there?'
Because a minister of Christ put them there.
'Why did he put them there?'
Because Christ commanded us from the beginning to do this in remembrance of him.

This means that at least part of what I think while I eat and drink is, 'I am eating this bread and drinking this wine. I am touching and feeling these physical things because Jesus, the real image of God, was a real man who lived on this earth and took real bread and wine and told me to remember him in them.'

God has given us his Holy Spirit. And by that Spirit we know him and become like him. But we are also bodies and need a tangible focus for our devotion and commitment to him. There are times when the things of the Spirit are shadowy and insubstantial. Perhaps you are going through a rebellious patch; perhaps a leader at your church is behaving badly; perhaps there are very few Christians around you showing the life of God in love and joy. Never mind. The bread is on the table and it is offered to you again and again in an unchangeable way. This is the sign of God's steadfast love to you.

IDOLATRY AND THE SACRAMENT

But we must not neglect the warning of the second commandment. God has indeed given us a focus of his presence but it is *not* an image, an idol. It is not to be worshipped or venerated or carried about as an object of superstition. Idolatry has a sad history even inside the Christian Church.

At the beginning of the Christian Church, the Jewish influence made it unthinkable that anyone would make even a representation of Christ. But from the fifth century, especially in the East, it became the fashion to make icons, that is images of Christ, and to use them in public and private worship. In the Greek church, they are treated with superstitious reverence with worshippers bowing before them and kissing them. In the Western church, the erection of images in churches was slower to develop but the idolatry which grew up in connection with the reserved sacrament was widespread.

At the Reformation in the sixteenth century, these idolatries and superstitions were rightly repudiated together with all the priest-craft associated with such views. It certainly is not biblical religion for a priest to claim that he can, with God's power, actually change the bread into the Body of Christ, and that this bread could then be exhibited to the people as an object for worship. But while we are right to reject the abuse of the sacraments we are not right to neglect them altogether nor to devalue them as some do. Certainly we must avoid idolatry, but we must use the sacraments for their God-appointed function.

I believe that if we ignore this bodily side of human life we become distorted. While we are called to exercise discipline in controlling our bodily desires we are not called to asceticism. An ascetic is an austere man who virtually denies there can be any good in the body at all. John the Baptist lived an ascetic life but Jesus was glad to enjoy the good simple pleasures of the body. Some Christians so spiritualise the Christian life that they forget that the God who is the Spirit is also the creator of everything and has given us all things that we may enjoy them. The truth of Christ becoming a man in a body and the truth of the sacraments are reminders that God wants to fill us, to forgive us and to enrich us in every aspect of life, bodily as well as spiritually.

SACRAMENTS OF THE GOSPEL

What, then, is the proper function of the sacraments? Both Baptism and Communion are sacraments of the gospel.[1] I referred in Chapter 2 to 'Word and Sacrament'; the two go naturally together.

The service of Communion contains ritual actions and ceremony.

If we are to know the significance of an action it must be accompanied by words. If you were a foreigner and knew no English nor Christianity and wandered into a Communion service you would see people putting money into a plate which is then presented to a leader at the front. Later on you would see that leader giving the people bread and wine and could easily conclude that it was some kind of eating-house. So the words are all important: they give meaning to the actions. The word which properly accompanies the sacraments is the gospel. By this I mean much more than reading out some verses from Matthew, Mark, Luke or John. I mean the basic teaching of Christianity such as I have outlined in Chapters 1–6. Thus, in the words of Article 25

sure witnesses . . . signs of grace . . . strengthen and confirm our faith in him.

You will find expressed in the Anglican Prayer Book services confession, forgiveness, grace, faith, commitment, love, obedience, hope and so on – in fact all the truths of the gospel.

But why should there be two sacraments and not one? There is, after all, only one gospel. The reason for this is that in the Bible, God's salvation is talked about in two ways. In some places it is presented as complete and finished. In others it is talked of as something we are still entering into and only beginning to enjoy. For instance, in Ephesians 2:5, 8 Paul says, 'By God's grace you have been saved' in the past tense. Indeed in Ephesians 1:4 he says that we were chosen 'before the world was made'! But on the other hand in Romans 13:11 Paul writes, 'For the moment when we *will* be saved is closer now than it was when we first believed.' Here salvation is talked about in a future tense, as something we have yet to possess. Different pictures are used to underline this double way of talking about the Christian life. In one place Paul says that being a Christian is like being adopted into a family. An adoption is a decisive act in the past. It is complete and final. Elsewhere he says that being a Christian is like running a race and that you have not finished yet. Your Christian life is still incomplete.

So your grasp of God's promises to you can be described as both complete and incomplete. The 'complete' descriptions use words to describe your status before God: re-born, adopted, justified, redeemed, passed from death to life, reconciled. These words assure you that you are safe and that God's love is irrevocable. But the 'incomplete' words remind you that life is dynamic and moving: walking, running, fighting, wrestling, working. Your sense of certainty should never allow you to become lazy; rather it should spur you to greater efforts.

How important it is to understand that this two-aspect view of God's salvation is quite different from a two-stage view of it. There are some churchmen who speak of a gift of regeneration at Baptism and then a gift of the Holy Spirit, at confirmation. How mistaken this view is can be seen when you realise that you cannot be born again without God's Holy Spirit. And then there are others who speak of first 'receiving Jesus' at conversion and then at a later time 'being baptised with the Holy Spirit.' I shall say more about this in the next chapter. It is enough to say here that Baptism signifies all the blessings of Christ in the Gospel to us completely, while Communion signifies our need increasingly to enjoy the blessings of Christ in the Gospel.

There is one other thing that the sacraments have in common. They both make central the death and resurrection of Jesus. This is because the New Testament makes the death and resurrection of Jesus central to our enjoyment of salvation. Let me expound this further.

HOLY BAPTISM

By our baptism then, we were buried with Christ and shared his death, in order that as he was raised from death by the glorious power of the Father, so also we might live a new life.   *Romans 6:4*

The symbolism is clear. The man to be baptised goes under the water, a picture of death: he then comes out of the water, a picture of a new life. Jesus went under the 'water' of death and then rose again with the life of the Spirit. So our baptism identifies us with Jesus, crucified and risen. A clean break with the past: there is now a new man.

There is the notion of *washing*: you are cleansed, forgiven your sins because of the death of Jesus. There is the idea of being *born again*, because you are starting a new life. There is the idea of *initiation*, because you are baptised into the body of Christ. And so you have become a *child of God* and *an inheritor* of all that God will give you in eternity with Christ. But the primary notion is that you are now identified with Christ. Your life is wrapped up with his life.

You are committed to him and he to you and nothing can change it. Baptism, then, is the sacrament of God's complete salvation *which is already yours* if you trust in him. That is why you can only be baptised once.

Sometimes when a young person is converted he wants to be baptised again because it is argued he was not conscious nor converted at the ceremony when he was a baby of six months. But he does not need to be re-baptised. After all, if he really is a Christian then he was chosen by God 'before the world was made', certainly before he was baptised as a baby.

HOLY COMMUNION

In Communion we have the double symbolism of bread and wine; of body and blood.

First, the wine. We have the significance of this in Jesus's own words.

This is my blood, which seals God's covenant, my blood poured out for many for the forgiveness of sins. *Matthew 26:28*

There are two ideas here. First, there is the certainty of God's offer and promise. In the Old Testament, the Covenant of God was ratified in a blood ceremony where half was sprinkled on the altar and half was sprinkled on the people. This signified the binding of the two parties God and Man. God does not break his promise easily; it is as strong as death. So the new promise, or New Covenant, is sealed with Christ's blood ... Nothing can change that! Secondly, by linking the idea of blood with the Old Testament sacrifices, the wine becomes a symbol of atonement, of complete forgiveness of sin. In this sense the wine is a picture of the continual cleansing that is needed by the Christian.

Thirdly, the bread. There is a rich symbolism here which is not easily simplified. In the first place the broken body, like the poured out wine, is a symbol of violent *death*. The separation of the pieces brings to mind the animal cut up to seal a covenant in Old Israel. This then is the body of Christ broken for us.

But then in John 6, Jesus repeatedly speaks of himself as 'the bread of life' and says 'whoever eats me will live because of me' (John 6:57). It is clear that this 'eating' of Christ is a picture of us believing in him. So the bread is also the *life* of Jesus offered to us and our eating is an expression of our faith.

But there is a third way in which we can understand the picture of the broken bread.

The bread which we break, is it not a communion in the body of Christ? Because there is one bread, we who are many, are one body, for we all partake of the one bread.   *I Corinthians 10:16, 17*

The body of Christ is another name for the Church; and so Paul applies it here in such a way that the sacrament becomes a picture of the diverse members of the Church being *one in Christ.*

Communion is thus also a picture of the unity of the Church in Christ and this is why you cannot celebrate communion on your own. You need the body of Christians in order to become mature in Christ yourself.

Communion is the sacrament of God's salvation which you need continually to appropriate and grow into. You should attend regularly. The discipline of the Church of England implies that this should be each Sunday and on Saints' Days, though the official direction is not less than three times a year, including Easter Day. 'At the Lord's Table with the Lord's people on the Lord's day' is a useful rule of life. It is, of course, a matter of personal judgment how often you think you need to be reminded of the central truths of the gospel.

SPIRIT AND SACRAMENT

I have not yet said exactly what sacraments are though I have already indicated why they are important.

A word I have frequently used is 'symbol' and I am going to follow that up for a moment. In Baptism, the symbolism is that I am identified with Christ in death and resurrection. In Communion, the bread and wine stand for the body and blood of Christ, that is Christ himself. And my eating and drinking and then digesting indicates how deep is to be my relationship with him. Like the vine and the branches there exists an organic union between Christ and the Christian. But how is this union to be effected? The union is effected by the Holy Spirit. Christ puts his Holy Spirit into me and this is what joins me to him. Baptism and Communion are both sacraments of the Holy Spirit.

Here are some words from the Baptism Service (Series II)

. . . by thy sending of the Spirit thou hast made us new men.   *Para 13* and from Paul

. . . all of us have been baptised into the one body by the same Spirit.

I Corinthians 12:13

Here are some words from the Communion Service (Series III in the new Anglican Liturgy)

The Lord is here
His Spirit is with us
. . . by the power of your spirit grant that these gifts of bread and wine may be to us his Body and his blood. . . .
. . . as we eat and drink . . . renew us by your Spirit. . . .

and from Paul

. . . and all have been given the one Spirit to drink.   *I Corinthians 10:4*

To the man who is truly repentant, believing and loving, the sacraments are not mere play-acting nor mere re-enacting, for the Holy Spirit is present to give reality to the body of Christ. There is no magic here, nor is there idolatry; but a real spiritual meeting between God and Man.

Let me put my point another way. The great Christian mystery is that a sinful, finite man can be joined to a holy, infinite God. No one will ever be able to explain or describe this mystery in plain terms. It is a great wonder and needs to be lived rather than described. I can write it like this:

GOD — HOLY SPIRIT — CHRISTIAN

Now there are some who want to include the sacrament of Holy Communion within this linked chain. They want to say that God joins himself to me by means of the Holy Spirit and that the Holy Spirit joins himself to me by means of bread and wine. They imply that the true picture is:

GOD — HOLY SPIRIT — BREAD/WINE — CHRISTIAN

and thus imply that the sacrament is another mystery in addition to the great mystery of the Christian. Those who teach such a view have made a basic category mistake. It would be like saying to a wife, 'Yes, I see you have two things: the promised love of your husband and a wedding ring.' But she would reply, 'No! I have one reality in my life: the promised love of my husband. This is expressed in many ways but in particular his love for me is embodied in this ring.' The sacrament is not a second mystery: it is a sacrament, a symbol, an embodiment, an expression of the great mystery. Any teaching on the sacraments which fails to give a central place to the work of the Holy Spirit is bound to fail for as Jesus said:

What gives life is God's Spirit; man's power is of no use at all. The words I have spoken to you are Spirit and life.   *John 6:63*

If I kiss my wife, then that physical meeting of the lips is an embodiment of my love for her. Of course, there may be pretence or hypocrisy. There may be kisses, like Judas's, which signify something else. But the real thing, a deep personal affection and commitment, is embodied in the genuine kiss.

Do not, then, in your Christian life, despise or neglect the sacraments. They can be the embodiment of your own commitment to God and God's declared unchangeable offer of himself to you, visible and tangible.

Note
1 You may care to read Article 25 of the 39 Articles of the Church of England. These Articles are still the expression of the official teaching of the Church of England.

Bible quotations for Chapter 8

THE CHRISTIAN IMAGE
(Christ) shines with the brightness of God's glory; he is the exact likeness of God's own being, and sustains the universe with his powerful word.   *Hebrews 1:3*

He is the image of the invisible God.   *Colossians 1:15 (RSV)*

All of us, then, reflect the glory of the Lord with uncovered faces; and that same glory, coming from the Lord who is the Spirit, transforms us into his very likeness, in an even greater degree of glory.   *II Corinthians 3:18*

A BODILY FOCUS

Go, then, to all peoples everywhere and make them my disciples: baptise them in the name of the Father, the Son and the Holy Spirit, and teach them to obey everything I have commanded you.   *Matthew 28:19, 20*

The Lord Jesus, on the night he was betrayed, took the bread, gave thanks to God, broke it. . . . 'Do this. . . .'   *1 Corinthians 11:23, 24*

NO IDOLATRY

My children, keep yourselves safe from false gods!   *1 John 5:21*

NO DEVALUING OF THE BODY

John the Baptist came, and he fasted and drank no wine, and you said, 'He is a madman!' The Son of Man came, and he ate and drank, and you said 'Look at this man! He is a glutton and a wine-drinker. . . .'   *Luke 7:33, 34*

. . . God, who generously gives us everything for us to enjoy.   *1 Timothy 6:17*

THE BLOOD

And Moses took the blood and threw it upon the people, and said, 'Behold the blood of the covenant which the Lord has made with you in accordance with all these words.'   *Exodus 24:8 (RSV)*

Indeed, according to the Law, almost everything is made clean by blood; and sins are forgiven only if blood is poured out.   *Hebrews 9:22*

THE BODY

This is my body which is broken for you.   *1 Corinthians 11:24 (RSV margin)*

I am the bread of life; he who comes to me shall not hunger.   *John 6:35 (RSV)*

CHRISTIAN LIFE

As for us, we have this large crowd of witnesses round us. Let us rid ourselves, then, of everything that gets in the way, and the sin which holds on to us so tightly, and let us run with determination the race that lies before us. Let us keep our eyes fixed on Jesus, on whom our faith depends from beginning to end.
                                                                Hebrews 12:1, 2

Questions for discussion

1   Is it possible to turn the Bible into an idol?

2   What do these words in the Series III Communion service mean: 'Through him you have made us a people for your own possession.'

3   What is the importance of Christian instruction for those who are baptised as babies?

9
Filled with the Spirit

'Why should I become a Christian?'

Because if you do, you will go to heaven when you die.

'How do I know I shall?'

Because Jesus promises everlasting life to all who believe in him.

'That sounds pretty dull, "everlasting life." Why should I want to go on living for ever and ever? Perhaps it would be better to be snuffed out like a candle. Besides I'm interested in life *now*, the real life that I know. It's difficult to work up enthusiasm for some life in the far future, in a place I can't understand and which you can't describe, or can you?'

Well not exactly describe it. You see, we shall have spiritual bodies.

'You mean you can see through them, like ghosts?'

It is not difficult to imagine such a conversation between a young Christian and his unbelieving friend. Everything that the Christian says is true and yet we must admit that the other is talking sense. Is that the Christian Difference: that we have a hope of everlasting life and the others do not? It should be obvious if you have followed me so far that, while this *is* part of the Difference, the main business of being a Christian is this life right now. Maybe after we have reached 'another place' this life will seem shadowy and unreal. But we are not there yet and the real challenge is how do you live at the moment?

EVERLASTING OR ETERNAL?

There is a difference in flavour between the words 'everlasting' and 'eternal.' The first does contain this notion of going on and on and on. And only God goes on and on, so only he can be said to be 'everlasting.' But if you think about it, that is to talk of God in terms of time, to say he has a past and a present and a future. Whereas the essence of God is that he is '*I am*' all the time. He is 'outside' time for he created it and the word 'eternal' catches this idea better. In the TEV translation 'eternal' is used in preference to the other and rightly so. Especially when you read repeatedly in John's gospel that Jesus offers 'eternal life' to men. An amazing offer because Jesus is saying that he can give you life of the same sort that God lives. And that you can have it now and not have to wait till heaven for it! Jesus said, 'I tell you the truth: whoever hears my words and believes in him who sent me, has eternal life. He will not be judged, but has already passed from death to life' (John 5:24). Note that word 'already.' It is clear that Jesus is not talking about physical death here, but a death of judgment or condemnation. Like a man under sentence of death. The moment he is pardoned he passes from 'death' to 'life.' Now he is released from the Law's demand he experiences a new kind of life.

Here is part of one of Jesus's prayers:

For you gave the Son authority over all men, so that he might give eternal life to all those you gave him. And this is eternal life: for men to know you, the only true God, and to know Jesus Christ, whom you sent.   *John 17:2, 3*

To know God, this is eternal life. 'Knowing,' of course, is much more than 'knowing about.' Like friends know each other and influence each other in their attitudes and actions, so to know God is to become like him.

Eternal life, then, is living with God and what a great encouragement this is! So many people look upon religion as something you do *for* God whereas at the centre of Christianity is the notion that it is something you do *with* God. It is a joint effort not just you struggling away on your own. It is true that God makes great demands on you: but he is alongside to provide the resources for you.

BECOMING A CHRISTIAN

If you believe in God the Father and God the Son and that is all, then Christianity is just another theology, another theory about God. But to believe in God the Holy Spirit is actually to receive God into your life. This means that God comes and shares his life with the believing Christian. Jesus spoke these words to his disciples:

I will ask the Father, and he will give you another Helper, the Spirit of truth, to stay with you forever. The world cannot receive him, because it cannot see him or know him. But you know him, for he remains with you and lives in you.

John 14:16, 17

You will see from these words that the whole Trinity is involved in the Holy Spirit coming to live in the Christian. It is the desire of the Son and the gift of the Father that you should have the Spirit for ever.

There are some preachers these days who are saying, 'When you become a Christian you asked Jesus into your heart. Now you must go a step further and ask for the Holy Spirit.' This advice rests on a theological muddle and it is important to get it straight. First it is true that the Bible writers sometimes talk of Christ living in our hearts, as, for instance, in Ephesians 3:17 '. . . that Christ will make his home in your hearts, through faith.' *But Christ does this by his Holy Spirit.* Another name for the Holy Spirit is 'the spirit of Christ' (Romans 8:9). When Jesus says, 'My Father and I will come to him and live with him' (John 14:23) then this is another way of talking about the gift of the Spirit, for the Spirit is both the Spirit of God and the Spirit of Jesus. God the Father could not be contained in heaven and earth, so he comes to live with us by his Spirit. Jesus the man who walked this earth is ascended into heaven, so he cannot be present to us except by his Spirit. It is therefore inaccurate and misleading to suggest that 'receiving Christ' and 'receiving the Holy Spirit' could be two different experiences. There are no first-class and second-class Christians; some who have received the Holy Spirit and some who have not. You cannot be a Christian at all, unless you have received the Holy Spirit: and if you have received the Holy Spirit then you are a Christian.

The Athanasian Creed puts the matter directly:

So likewise the Father is Lord, the Son Lord: and the Holy Ghost Lord. And yet not three Lords but one Lord.

We do not believe in three Gods, nor in a three-headed God. But the Father is Lord overall and the Son is the Lord in person and the Spirit is the Lord who is present to us to command us, direct us and change us to be like himself.

The Spirit is self-effacing. Jesus said, 'he will speak about me'

(John 15:26) so it is not surprising that preachers preach Christ and offer Christ to the hearers. That is fine as long as no one tries to separate Christ and the Spirit into two Lords who come to the believer at different times and bring different experiences.

FULLNESS OF THE SPIRIT

The important command in Ephesians 5:18: 'be filled with the Spirit' is sometimes misunderstood. The meaning of the language could be better expressed, 'Go on being filled with the Spirit' for you do not get filled once and that is that. It is a continual activity.

If you have in your mind a picture of a glass being filled with water then of course it stays full until it is used up. This is a static picture of man and of the Spirit. It implies, though it is rarely spelled out like this, that man is a static container of some kind and that the Spirit is a liquid which can either be used up or which evaporates. Jesus does use water as a picture of the Spirit, but he emphasises that it is *living* water (*ie* running water). And the word that is used for 'Spirit' can also mean 'breath' or 'wind.'

Therefore to talk about 'being filled with the Spirit' is to talk about an activity where the Christian and the Holy Spirit share the same aims, love and power. If, in sinning, the Christian suddenly diverges from the Spirit's activity, then he is no longer in the Spirit and certainly he is not filled. This does not mean that the Spirit goes away for he stays to convict the sin. But what this means is that you cannot talk about being filled with the Spirit once and for all. Being filled with the Spirit is a daily, an hourly doing what God wants. Rather than a static glass of water, think of a sail of a boat filled with wind. The wind of the Spirit never stops blowing but by inept handling the sail can be empty and therefore the boat is powerless.

THE KING AND I

What is it that happens then, when the Lord who is the Spirit comes to me? What can he do for me? Paul writes in II Timothy 1:7: 'For the Spirit that God has given us does not make us timid: instead his Spirit fills us with power. . . .' In Chapter 5, I spoke of the drastic revolution that must take place if I am going to change my 'human nature' or self-centredness. I shall certainly need *power* to do this. By definition I cannot find this power from within myself, for my own personal power is all dedicated to my self-advancement. But the Spirit can give me power to overcome my self and leave self behind. This is a strange experience and one which is very difficult to explain to an unbeliever. The outsider looking at the Christian may think him to be a very strong-minded person but the inside story is different. The Christian knows himself to be as weak as water and that the power-secret of his life is the same as that of Paul:

Finally, build up your strength in union with the Lord and by means of his mighty power. *Ephesians 6:10*

Young Christians often fear that they will 'never keep it up.' And they are right. They will never by themselves keep up the fight against sin and the struggle to build a God-like character. But being a Christian means that you have received the Spirit of power. It is now up to you to claim and use that power.

Secondly, the Spirit because he is the *Holy* Spirit will show me where I am wrong and sinful. 'When he comes he will convince the world of sin. . . .' (John 16:8 RSV). Of course, non-Christians have a conscience and know when they are wrong. But the Christian's conscience is both educated and sensitised by the Spirit's presence. When a new Christian suddenly says, 'I think I spend too much time playing tennis,' it is not that tennis is sinful, nor has he heard a sermon on the evils of playing tennis. It is that the Spirit is teaching him to look at his life with new eyes and new priorities. The Spirit will certainly be quick to point out behaviour that is sinful. This is not particularly comfortable and can make the Christian sad. But it is a proper, not a morbid sorrow and provided that it leads to repentance it can be health-giving. It is also very likely that a positive command comes with the negative prohibition. For instance, it might be 'Less tennis: more Sunday School teaching' or 'Less money spent on make-up means more money given to famine relief.'

Thirdly, it is the Spirit who makes us sure in our inward minds that we truly do belong to God and enjoy his favour. Many new Christians are plagued by doubt and uncertainty:

'Am I truly accepted by God?'

'Am I really born again and have I really a new life in Christ?'

'Can I be sure my sins are forgiven?'

'Will I go to heaven?'

The answer to such doubts is to hear God's word about the work of God's spirit:

For the Spirit that God has given you does not make you a slave and cause you to be afraid; instead the Spirit makes you God's sons, and by the Spirit's power we cry to God, 'Father! my Father!' God's Spirit joins himself to our spirits to declare that we are God's children. *Romans 8:15, 16*

To be sure of salvation is the right of every Christian. It is not arrogant to say, 'I'm sure I'm going to heaven.' It is God's intention that you should be sure and that is why he has given you his Spirit.

A DAILY WALK

Having just stated the truth that the Christian life is complete and sure in the Spirit, let me also state the complementary truth that you must daily keep your relationship with God in good repair. After all every baby is alive and secure in his relationship to his mother but she still takes great care to nourish that baby daily. So Paul urges us to walk according to the Spirit and Jesus says we should follow him *daily*.

The best way to nourish your Christian life is by setting aside a time each day to read the Bible and to pray. Again the work of God's Spirit is of central importance. For the Scriptures are inspired, that is God has breathed into them by his Spirit. The individual authors of the books of the Bible have in many cases stamped their own personalities on their writings. Nevertheless the books each in their own way reveal God. Never read the Bible without first asking the Holy Spirit to show you what *he* has written there.

The Spirit searches everything, even the hidden depths of God's purposes. . . .
Only God's Spirit knows all about God. . . .
We have received the Spirit sent by God, that we may know all that God has given us. . . . *I Corinthians 2:10, 11, 12*

When you pray, the Spirit himself prompts you and helps you to pray. At times it can be very difficult and it is a struggle to go on. Pause and ask the Spirit to help you pray.

This daily time of quiet conversation with God is something that Christians have found to be of great use. The tradition of Daily Offices, like Morning and Evening Prayer in the Anglican Prayer Book, goes back for centuries. Whether you use formal or informal prayer does not greatly matter. What does matter is that you live your life with God day by day.

THE KING AND US

In his letter Paul uses the phrase 'in Christ' or its equivalent 'in the Lord' 164 times. That is what the Spirit does for us; he places us 'in Christ' and especially 'into the body of Christ.' I wrote in Chapter 2 that the Christian experience is corporate and this is a great truth being brought before us in these days. '(We) have all been baptised into the one body by the same Spirit, and we have all been given the one Spirit to drink' (I Corinthians 12:13). The work of the Spirit among Christians is to bring unity and mutual love. If you find that there is division in a group or gossiping or bickering then this is evidence that the Holy Spirit is not being allowed to have his way.

Sometimes in a church there is a division between the older, more conventional group and the younger go-ahead and let's-all-relax group. It is the same Spirit that lives in both and it is up to all the Christians to see that the unity of the Spirit is given a chance to work out. Thoughtless generalisations ('That's typical of those young people') and blanket disapprovals ('Well what else do you expect from people who've lived here for thirty years?') could never be spoken by God who made all men.

Or sometimes there is a social division between the professional white-collar member of the Church and the working man. God knows no such distinction between men. Riches mean nothing to him and every social grouping for him is based on artificial differences. Clearly, then, if we treat people according to their outward appearance, we are guilty of sin.

In some churches there has been division over the question of the gifts of the Spirit. Perhaps one group has the gift of speaking in tongues while another has a gift of doing more conventional Bible study. You would think that when Christians were specially thinking about the work of the Spirit in their lives that it would draw them all very close to each other. Yet it has been the bitter experience of some that the old nature has driven out the Spirit and despising and division have come instead. 'To have your mind controlled by what human nature wants will result in death; to have your mind controlled by what the Spirit wants will result in life and peace.'

Never forget, then, that it is not just 'the King and I'; it is also 'the King and us.' It is obviously vital for your own existence as a Christian that the Holy Spirit lives in you, fashioning your attitudes, empowering your actions, guiding your decisions. But your maturity as a Christian also demands that you are continually relating to and loving that body of Christ into which the Spirit draws you.

WHY SOME FAIL

'Demas fell in love with this present world and has deserted me' (II Timothy 4:10). Ever since Paul's time Christians have had the sadness of seeing some of the Church deserting the fellowship. Will it be you? Of course it need not be you but none of us is so strong that we can afford to ignore the warnings.

In the Book of Common Prayer we are told that our enemies are 'the World, the Flesh and the Devil,' and in the Litany we have some reminders of the ways in which we can fall. I have talked quite a lot about the world in Chapter 6, but what about 'the flesh'? When 'flesh' is contrasted with 'Spirit' it means the old human nature especially the pride of self-righteousness. But 'flesh' can also refer to the basic sins connected with bodily appetite: too much drinking, too much eating, forbidden sexual relationships, self-indulgence of all kinds including getting up too late in the morning. It is surprising how often one of these fundamental sins brings a man down and deadens his spiritual response to God. It is even more surprising that some particular sins, especially loose sexuality, are labelled 'immoral' while others like over-eating are socially acceptable within the Church. The rule is, be guided by the Word of God and not by the tradition of men.

Those who try to counsel people mixed up with Satanism are only too aware of the personal character of the powers of evil. But even in the ordinary run of the Christian life, one can easily feel the weight of the adversary, or the accuser, as his name means. The book of Revelation reminds us that the struggle on earth between good and evil is only an aspect of the cosmic battle that is going all the time between Christ and the devil. One practical implication of this teaching is the reminder that you have an adversary who is stronger than you, even though he is weaker than Christ: a reminder that you *cannot* live the Christian life without Christ's Holy Spirit, a fact we are continually tempted to forget. If often we are unaware directly of Satan's presence it is because of the mercy of God which restrains him.

I think I have also become aware of the devil's activity in the world structures. For example: social class divisions; employers' passion for profits; Unions' preoccupation with wage-claims; privilege which grips a whole section of society and is self-perpetuating; world sales of arms; the doctrine of success; the alienation of large sections of the working class from the Church; racialism; the pride of education and intellectualism. You can understand all these things but at times they have a demonic feel about them, as though a group were being ruled by a collective obsession. 'I write to you, young men, because you are strong; the word of God lives in you and you have defeated the Evil One' (I John 2:14).

In the parable of the soils, Jesus categorised the failures as follows:

● Those from whom the devil snatched the Word of God away before anything could happen at all. These comprise an enormous group: men and women, boys and girls whose every serious thought can be blotted out by the next television programme or whatever happens to catch their fancy. The warning is clear: if you get a jolt from the Spirit of Truth, be sure to listen!

● Those who had no root and withered away under the onslaught of difficulty. When trouble or persecution comes, they give up at once. How important are those words in the Baptism service '. . . continue as Christ's faithful soldier and servant unto his life's end.' The book of Hebrews is full of encouragement to persevere: read it through if you are weakening. Life is often hard work and there will come times when everything, including your Christian experience, goes stale on you. 'Hang on! Keep at it. Don't give up,' says Jesus. In the Luke version (8:15) it says,

The seed that fell in good soil stands for those who hear the message and retain it in a good and obedient heart, and persist until they bear fruit.

How much we need Christians who will persist when sins crowd in, when disaster strikes, when routine deadens, when the adversary attacks, and when life is just dull! He that endures to the end shall be saved.

● Those whose Christian lives are described as 'choked.' Here the threat is more subtle. The plant is left to grow but other plants and thistles grow beside it and slowly throttle the true crop. Suppose a young man of twenty gives his life to Christ and survives the immediate and obvious temptations. In the next twenty years as he grows into middle-age other things will crowd in on him: he will get more responsibility and he will probably get richer. Certainly he will acquire more possessions. These two things 'cares' and 'riches' will be enough to choke his walk with the Holy Spirit. Persistence here will mean steady, continual weeding and pruning, and to be honest, relatively few Christian men are prepared for this kind of commitment. Slowly they become ineffective and some, like Demas, desert altogether.

Would that all Christians would heed the warnings. The Prayer Book warns us against false doctrine, heresy, schism, hardness of heart and contempt of God's word and commandment. Jesus says,

Be careful then, how you listen; for whoever has something will be given more, but whoever has nothing will have taken away from him even the little he thinks he has.   *Luke 8:18*

THE SATISFACTION OF LOVE
Let us finish on a positive note: the Holy Spirit is given to us that we might be full of love – free, open, unashamed, relentless love. This love is the very life of God and we have been promised eternal life for ourselves. It is loving that makes us happy for it means finding the centre of our lives *outside* ourselves. Let's face it, we have tried for long enough to get happiness by being self-centred and we know it does not work. So let the Holy Spirit drive you out in attitude and action and find your destiny in being a Servant. It doesn't sound much fun but that is because we are still imprisoned in the old closed way. Try it for yourself. Let the Holy Spirit pour out his love through you and you will experience eternal life. You will be different and the difference will be Christian.

Bible quotations for Chapter 9

FILLED WITH THE SPIRIT
Listen to this secret: we shall not all die, but in an instant we shall all be changed, as quickly as the blinking of an eye, when the last trumpet sounds. For when it sounds, the dead will be raised immortal beings, and we shall all be changed.
I Corinthians 15:51, 52

BECOMING A CHRISTIAN
(Jesus said,) Whoever loves me will obey my message. My Father will love him and my Father and I will come to him and live with him. *John 14:23*

Whoever does not have the Spirit of Christ does not belong to him. *Romans 8:9*

FULLNESS OF THE SPIRIT
They were all filled with the Holy Spirit and began to talk in other languages . . .
Acts 2:4

(and then, later, of the same group)When they finished praying, the place where they were meeting was shaken. They were all filled with the Holy Spirit and began to speak God's message with boldness. *Acts 4:31*

THE KING AND I
And when he (the Spirit) comes he will prove to the people of the world that they are wrong about sin, and about what is right, and about God's judgment.
John 16:8

I have been put to death with Christ on his cross, so that it is no longer I who live, but it is Christ who lives in me. This life that I live now, I live by faith in the Son of God, who loved me and gave his life for me. *Galatians 2:19, 20*

. . . we look forward to possess the rich blessings that God keeps for his people. He keeps them for you in heaven, where they cannot decay or spoil or fade away. They are for you, who through faith are kept safe by God's power as you wait for the salvation which is ready to be revealed at the end of time. *I Peter 1:4, 5*

A DAILY WALK
This book of the law shall not depart out of your mouth, but you shall meditate on it day and night, that you may be careful to do according to all that is written in it; for then you shall make your way prosperous and then you shall have good success. *Joshua 1:8 (RSV)*

(Jesus said,) Think not that I have come to abolish the law and the prophets (*ie* the Old Testament); I have come not to abolish them but to fulfil them.
Matthew 5:17 (RSV)

Be joyful always, pray at all times, be thankful in all circumstances.
I Thessalonians 5:16–18

THE KING AND US

... if I have not love, I am nothing. ... if I have not love, it does me no good. Love never gives up ... Love is eternal ... Meanwhile these three remain: faith, hope and love; and the greatest of these is love.   *I Corinthians 13*

If you have love for one another, then all will know that you are my disciples.
John 13:35

WHY SOME FAIL

For we are not fighting against human beings, but against the wicked spiritual forces in the heavenly world.   *Ephesians 6:12*

The one who thinks he is standing up had better be careful that he does not fall.
I Corinthians 10:12

Be alert, stand firm in the faith, be brave, be strong.   *I Corinthians 16:13*

Keep watch, and pray, so you will not fall into temptation. The spirit is willing, but the flesh is weak.   *Matthew 26:41*

THE SATISFACTION OF LOVE

Happy are those whose greatest desire is to do what God requires:
God will satisfy them fully!   *Matthew 5:6*

Questions for discussion

1 If the Spirit of God is also the Spirit of Jesus what does this imply about who Jesus is?

2 How would you advise a new Christian who felt unsure of his position in God's sight?

3 What does the Christian have to hope for?